REPRESENTATION
IN ITALY

REPRESENTATION IN ITALY

*Institutionalized Tradition
and Electoral Choice*

SAMUEL H. BARNES

THE UNIVERSITY OF CHICAGO
PRESS
Chicago & London

SAMUEL H. BARNES was named chairman of the Department of Political Science in 1977 and is program director, Center for Political Studies, ISR, at the University of Michigan. He is the author of *Party Democracy* and numerous articles. He is currently coordinating an eight-nation survey project on expectations and political action.

THE UNIVERSITY OF CHICAGO PRESS, CHICAGO 60637
THE UNIVERSITY OF CHICAGO PRESS, LTD., LONDON
© 1977 by The University of Chicago
All rights reserved. Published 1977
Printed in the United States of America
81 80 79 78 77   9 8 7 6 5 4 3 2 1

Chapter 7 is based upon and figure 4 and tables 25 and 28 were originally published in "Left, Right, and the Italian Voter," *Comparative Political Studies* 4 (October 1971): 157–75 (Sage Publications, Inc.).

Library of Congress Cataloging in Publication Data

Barnes, Samuel Henry, 1931–
    Representation in Italy.

    Includes bibliographical references and index.
    1. Representative government and representation—
Italy.   2. Italy—Politics and government—1945–
3. Elections—Italy.   I. Title.
JN5477.R4B37   320.9'45'092   76-51819
ISBN 0-226-03726-6

Contents

Preface   *ix*

1. *Representation in Perspective*   *1*
2. *The Parties and the Institutionalization of Tradition*   *17*
3. *The Italian Electoral System*   *33*
4. *Traditions, Networks, and Social Structure*   *41*
5. *Continuities in Partisanship*   *65*
6. *Political Involvement*   *78*
7. *Attitudes—Left and Right*   *97*
8. *Representatives and the Represented*   *116*
9. *Representatives and Parties*   *135*
10. *Representation in Italy—and Beyond*   *156*

Appendix—*The Design of the Study*   *161*
Notes   *167*
Index   *183*

For E. L. B. and F. B.

Preface

This monograph on Italy is one of a series of studies on representation in individual countries, carried out by colleagues at the University of Michigan. These studies share most features of a common research design that includes interviews with a national mass sample and with a sample of candidates to the dominant house of the national legislature. The common design features will permit subsequent cross-national analyses; Italy is our focus in this volume.

A timeless portrayal of contemporary Italian politics is an impossibility: All eras may be transitional from some perspective, but 1968 in Italy looms as a watershed year, one in which the patterns visible since the immediate postwar years began to fade. Of course, 1968 was merely a year of acceleration of that process of movement that is perpetual in societies. Moreover, the magnitude of change cannot yet be assessed. In 1977, and more than thirty years after the imprinting of the patterns analyzed in this book, Italy is still being governed not just by the same party but by the same individuals who were in control before 1950. Perhaps Hegel's Owl of Minerva does fly only at twilight; perhaps we can only understand an age when it is over. If this is true, this book is premature, for the old era is not yet dead and buried, and multiple alternative scenarios for the new era are just now appearing; unlike in the movies, the definitive script will only be written in retrospect.

Thus, 1968 was a good year in which to study representation in Italy. The patterns presented in this book began to blur at that time; new ones are not yet in focus. For that reason I decided not to update these findings with more recent surveys and political developments. The data base for the three-tiered analysis utilized here is unique; *aggiornamento* will require not only equally good data but also an equally well-established pattern to analyze.

Before thanking the many people and institutions that assisted me, I wish to express my regrets about two important resources that I was unable to exploit. Professor Giuseppe DiPalma's research on the policy process in the Italian parliament (*Surviving Without Governing: The Italian Parties in Parliament*, Berkeley and Los Angeles: University of California Press, forthcoming) complements the "outside" model treated in the present work. This manuscript became available only after mine had been completed. The second undertaking that would have been relevant is the research on the Italian parliament being undertaken by a team directed by Professor Alberto Predieri of the University of Florence. Publications from this project were also not available until this volume was completed.

The interviews with the deputies and the mass sample were made possible by a grant for representation studies from the Ford Foundation to the University of Michigan. The councilor interviews were supported by research funds of the Horace H. Rackham School of Graduate Studies of the University of Michigan. Another grant for Latin political studies from the Ford Foundation to the Center for Political Studies sustained the analysis phase of the study. I spent the academic year 1967–68 in Rome as a visiting lecturer under the auspices of the American Commission for Cultural Exchanges with Italy. I am grateful to all of these institutions for their assistance in this project.

A number of people contributed to the pleasure as well as the success of this enterprise. Dr. Frank Casale took part in the project from its inception until well into the analysis phase; his intelligence, diligence, and friendship in Ann Arbor and in Rome will remain among the fondest memories of these times. Alberto Spreafico, now *Ordinario* at the University of Catania, was, as always, a generous advisor, collaborator, and friend. Dottoressa Cipriana Scelba, Director of the American Commission for Cultural Exchanges with Italy, was helpful in many ways while I was a visiting lecturer at the University of Rome in 1967–68 and at other times. Professor Giovanni Sartori, then *Ordinario* at the University of Florence and now at Stanford University, was a pioneer in the study of representation in Italy; his counsel has been invaluable. Professor Gianni Statera of the University of Rome has been very kind to this visiting scholar, in 1967–68 and since.

The field research was executed by CISER (Centro Italiano di Studi e

Ricerche) of Rome. Dott. Sergio Lieto, its director, and his staff were excellent collaborators, both professionally and personally.

Several people have assisted with the data analyses. In addition to Dr. Casale, I want to single out Peter Joftis, Barbara Farah, and Michael-john Morgan. A series of wonderful secretaries have typed portions of the manuscript: I am especially grateful to Margaret Atkins, Margot Van Dis, and Garland Montalvo.

I have benefited tremendously from my association with stimulating and creative associates in the Center for Political Studies, the Michigan Department of Political Science, and the field of comparative politics. The modern study of representation was pioneered by my colleague, Warren Miller, and my former colleague, Donald Stokes, and they also took part in this cross-national representation project. Warren Miller's critique is especially appreciated; his suggestions after a thorough and prompt reading of the manuscript delayed its completion but added immensely to its value. I have also profited from critical readings by Ronald Inglehart, Robert Leonardi, Kenneth Organski, and Giacomo Sani. Needless to say, the weaknesses in the volume are the fault of the author and not of his colleagues.

Anne, Christopher, Michael, and Cathy helped by sharing my love of Italy and in many other ways. This book is dedicated to my father, Eugene L. Barnes, and to the memory of my father-in-law, Frank Bivona— exemplary representatives of their traditions.

1

Representation in Perspective

This is a study of political representation in Italy at a particular historical moment: It focuses on the process of representation at the time of the 1968 legislative elections. It also builds on the established tradition of theory and empirical research in the study of elite-mass linkages. Our data deal only with Italy; our goal is to examine representation in Italy within a broader perspective.

Representation is a concept encrusted with diverse meanings by a long, turbulent, and varied history. It is a "Protean" concept, in Loewenberg's words, and can be dealt with on several levels.[1] The metaphysical dimension involves the analysis of the fundamental conceptions of man and the universe represented in particular civilizations.[2] This dimension is highly relevant in Italy where the process of representation involves a cleavage that reflects deep philosophical differences. In addition, representation has a historical-theoretical dimension—what representation has meant in the past and present— which is the concern of historians, political theorists, and sociologists of knowledge.[3] Finally, there is the empirical-behavioral dimension of representation.[4] It deals with the relationships between representatives and the represented in particular polities at particular times. These levels of analysis are cumulative, in that the more general encompasses the less general; they are levels of abstraction, not discrete categories.

Although we focus on the empirical-behavioral level, the other levels are important for the contemporary process of representation in Italy.

1

Topics such as the changing meaning of representation in Italian history, the ideological roots of the various Italian political traditions, and the different meanings of representation for the various traditions are all relevant. Even at the empirical-behavioral level, representation is eternally intertwined with normative themes; no approach will satisfy everyone. Nevertheless, in the pages that follow we will sketch out a perspective on representation that we believe will improve the usefulness of the concept for comparative analyses.

None of the many existing definitions of representation meets our needs. For example, de Grazia calls it "a relation between two persons, the representative and the represented or constituent, with the representative holding the authority to perform various actions that incorporate the agreement of the represented."[5] While de Grazia rightly focuses on the notion of representation as a *relationship,* he does not include a role for the party or other associations as intermediaries in the process. We agree with Sartori that "citizens in modern democracies are represented *through* and *by* parties," and that "the role of the party as an intervening variable has remained a neglected area of research."[6] Representation involves elite-mass linkages. Yet, as Eulau and Prewitt insist, the existence of such linkages does not guarantee that "representation" takes place.[7] Representation emerges from these linkages, as they put it, when representatives "act in political ways *responsive* to the preferences expressed by the public, or groups and sectors within the public, and select programs and adopt policies in general accordance with those preferences."[8] Thus representation is something that is present or absent in varying degrees.

We believe that representation is a dimension of mobilization and consequently takes place in many ways—through contacts between the citizen and representatives of the administration as well as of the parliament, through organizations such as unions as well as parties, through politicians' responses to public opinion polls as well as to electoral results—in short, in any linkage that involves political elites being responsive to the preferences of the public or some part of it. A thorough study of representation would therefore have to examine all aspects of these linkages; it would have to examine the entire process of political mobilization.

ON MOBILIZATION

We view representation as a dimension of mobilization.[9] In our own conceptualization, mobilization is the development of linkages between elite and mass that relate both to the pursuit of systemic goals.[10]

Mobilization may also involve people in the *formulation* as well as the *pursuit* of goals, but this is not a necessary condition, for people may take part in the latter without the former. Political participation, in its conventional formulations by Milbrath and Verba and Nie, is one form of mobilization and the most commonly analyzed in Western democracies.[11] But mobilization may not be political at all in its outward forms, though we would argue that it always has political implications. For example, more people have been mobilized by religious movements than by parties: Who would deny the vast political ramifications of this form of mobilization? And economic transformations that have broken up the little communities of the world and have involved people in ever larger and more complex economic undertakings have in recent centuries been the most dramatic mobilizers of all. Yet, political participation historically lagged far behind economic and social mobilization, at least in Western Europe and North America. Political mobilization is therefore not synonymous with political participation, for the former is possible without the latter.

Mobilization can take many forms. For example, it is a wonder of our times that so many people have been induced by the media and other forms of communication to abandon localism, subsistence economic existence, and political apathy in order to involve themselves in the massive transformations of our age. And economic mobilization has resulted from the disruption of old societies, technological innovation, the expansion of a market economy, colonialism, and the growing interconnectedness of economic life. It is such a pervasive form of mobilization that it is often equated—we think wrongly—with mobilization in general. We say wrongly because there is no necessary connection between economic and political mobilization. While Western societies had widespread economic mobilization before extensive political mobilization got under way, the success of Leninist-type parties in mobilizing an economically backward peasantry in several parts of the world attests to the absence of temporal priorities in the process of mobilization. Consequently, it is incorrect to insist on a close relationship between the level of economic development and the level of mobilization. While such a relationship seems to exist for the Western democracies, it derives from the particular historical experiences of these societies and is not necessarily to be found everywhere.

Because mobilization as we have conceptualized it is a more general term than participation, we find it more useful for our purposes. We will restrict political participation to its more precise meaning of active citizen involvement in matters explicitly political. In this way we can better understand the part played by nonpolitical organizations and processes in tying people into their polities. In this study we will examine conventional forms of political participation. And we will also consider how religion, economic transformation, and education—to cite three obvious facilitators of mobilization—have served to develop linkages between elite and mass for the pursuit of societal goals even without the active political participation of individuals.

ON REPRESENTATION AS THE NORMATIVE DIMENSION OF MOBILIZATION

We have stated that representation is a dimension of mobilization. We can now specify which dimension it is: It is the normative dimension, the evaluative dimension, the dimension that deals with the *quality* of mobilization. For that reason, representation is, has been, and always will be a disputatious subject. This is because what *should* be represented in any particular polity at any particular time is a normative question. A good system of representation, like justice and beauty, lies in the eye of the beholder. But this does not mean that as scholars we have nothing to say about representation. We can articulate the criteria implicit in the expectations of different categories of people in different polities. And, given these criteria, we can evaluate the degree to which the polity meets them. While we cannot as political scientists determine what elite-mass linkages should be, we can evaluate the congruence between what people think they should be and what they are.

Congruence can exist along many dimensions. In the Anglo-American research tradition great emphasis has been placed on elite-mass congruence in policy preferences, congruence that has rather precise operational referents such as legislative votes, views on the issues of the day, and so on. This is indeed an important form of congruence in Western democracies; even there, however, its relevance is limited by the population's absence of opinions on many subjects and by the influence of elites and elite-dominated sources on mass preferences.

In many societies it is differences in general outlook rather than in specific policy preferences that form the lines along which congruence is sought. These differences may be ideological, or they may be traditional, involving religion, language, ethnicity, or local particularisms. While most traditional differences have ideological components, to classify them simply as ideological misses the richness and complexity of their public impact. Class is still another dimension along which differences may exist. In the Marxist tradition of analysis it is differences in material interests that are the stuff of politics, and hence it is these, when given concrete meaning in class terms, that should be the criteria of representation. Of course, there are other dimensions along which congruence can be evaluated; we have only suggested a few as examples. The important point is that what should be represented—and hence what should be evaluated for congruence—is itself an evaluative question, a normative issue. It is equally important that the question of what should be the lines of congruence, and consequently the basis for the evaluation of representation, is greatly affected by the lines of cleavage existing within a society. And what these lines really are is itself a complex question that must be confronted empirically for each country.

MOBILIZATION AND CONFLICT

Politics deals with conflict and its resolution. No conflict, no politics. At least, no politics that is of interest to us. And it is conflict over matters that alter the larger entity in some direct way that interests us, rather than interpersonal conflict that bears but remotely on general public policy. The latter form is ubiquitous; the former is undoubtedly latent in all societies, though not all societies admit its legitimacy and attempt to direct it into regular channels for resolution. When conflict recurs along the same lines it wears away the surface, so to speak, so that channels become cleavages into which future conflict tends to drain; and the deeper the cleavage the wider the range of issues that topple into it. This fact that conflict tends to recur in the same mode adds structure to politics and, indeed, institutionalizes it and often ritualizes it. And this has immense ramifications for representation.

Despite the existence of many similarities in the cleavage structures of contemporary polities, there are substantial disagreements within these polities over what the relevant lines of cleavage *should* be and consequently which cleavages should be recognized and legitimized in the polity.[12] Participants in the political game are usually stronger along some lines of cleavage than others, and they want to define the rules of the game so as to maximize their competitive advantage. In electoral games, the strategy is to try to focus the campaign on those issues on which you look good and the opposition looks bad. In the wider political game the strategy is the same. As a result, parties and social groups are unlikely to agree on what the real cleavages of society are.

It is tempting to state that the advantage of pluralistic polities is that the game is open and anybody can play, or at least anybody with some resources can play. Even in these polities the institutionalization of the rules of the game—which seems to be the source of the polities' stability and longevity—has the consequence of aiding some players and handicapping others. This is because a highly institutionalized polity forces players into strategies that may not enable them to perform as well as they might have done under other arrangements. The influence of a single-member district electoral system as compared with proportional representation and multiple members is an example, because it makes it more difficult to promote some cleavages than others.[13] An institutionalized political system tends to freeze the cleavage structure by facilitating the promotion of some forms of cleavage over others. Hence no polity can escape the problem of system bias. Different types of regimes systematically repress certain types of cleavage while admitting others, and the patterns that we discern reflect aspects of mobilization.

Traditional societies, for example, exhibit enforced consensus and lack of mobilization. In Putnam's words, "The elite extracts taxes and services from the nonelite but does not attempt to mobilize them for collective goals. Intra-elite conflict is personalistic and largely unrelated to broader social problems and tensions."[14] Even when there are deeply rooted cleavages between social groups, as in the traditional caste system of India, they may not lead to *political conflict*, because the cleavage is only marginally subject to political manipulation. Caste was once sanctioned, and few were concerned with whether those at the bottom really thought that it was just or unjust. It is precisely because traditional societies assume that whatever is, is right, that traditional societies seem to reflect so strongly personalistic politics and patron-client patterns of representation. There is no coming together of elites and mass for the definition and pursuit of common goals; one does what tradition has ordained one to do. The most blatant forms of cleavage, as between rich and poor, are denied political legitimacy; the myth of consensus is maintained.

The perpetuation of the myth is possible only insofar as the society is not mobilized.[15] Economic and other forms of growth seem to lead to group mobilization, and when this happens it becomes more and more difficult to maintain the fiction of consensus. But though it is difficult, it is not impossible. For it is a feature of authoritarian systems that many are able to provide the facade of mobilization without the reality. Individuals and even groups can be brought into the system—mobilized, if you will—but on a very selective basis so that the fiction of consensus can be maintained. It is somewhat of a surprise to students of mobilization that much change is compatible with the continuation of highly personalistic forms of politics; the patron-client system usually identified with traditional societies can in fact continue to exist for a very long time in a society with modern forms of economic and other organization.

Corporatist and pseudocorporatist patterns constitute an instructive form of mobilization. They seem especially relevant in Latin societies. Catholic social doctrines have been greatly influenced by corporatist thinking; papal encyclicals have suggested structures similar to corporatism as a preferred alternative to capitalism and socialism; several Latin Catholic countries have experimented with corporatism, though the seriousness of the institutional changes is open to question. Corporatism seems to be a useful device for authoritarian regimes to deal with limited mobilization; this is because corporatist patterns facilitate the tying in of new groups through highly particularistic arrangements made with concrete social categories. That is, accommodation may be achieved between traditional elites and new claimants, such as entrepreneurs or skilled workers or institutional intellectuals, without the system becoming either truly universalistic in its reward structure or extensively mobilized. In the corporatist system the state bureaucracy itself may be a major actor and not just the executor of elite decisions; the army may serve as the ultimate arbiter. Undoubtedly the Catholic emphasis on consensus and opposition to social conflict facilitate corporatist thinking. But retarded industrialization and the consequent absence of rapid social and economic change certainly render it easier for older elites everywhere to accommodate to newer groups. Until recent years, Latin countries had not experienced the thorough and relatively rapid social change that characterized the most industrialized countries in the last century; in its absence they have simply absorbed much of the new while retaining much of the old. Thus social groups that would be merely quaint fossils in other countries have remained politically important. As we will see in the next chapter, evolution has produced a geological spectacular in Italy.

There are many ways in which traditional patterns of elite-mass linkage can endure in an age of complex organizations. Corporatist patterns are one of these. Another is through devices that grant the appearance of mass mobilization with little of its substance, such as the charismatic demagogic figure in the pseudomass movement. It is not surprising that Italy under fascism combined corporatism, the leader, and the pseudomass movement in an attempt to maintain the status quo in an age crying out for mass mobilization.

7

Finally, patron-client patterns of politics are another way to prolong traditional patterns of linkage. They remained very important in republican Italy and merit a brief discussion because of their implications for the analysis of cleavage.

Patron-client relationships have been observed in diverse settings, and a substantial literature attests to their near-universal existence as well as their adaptability to several types of economic systems and levels of development.[16] They exist throughout the Mediterranean, in the political organizations of large American cities, in peasant societies throughout much of the world, and in old-boy networks of government and academia.

Although several varieties have been identified, the basic form is simple: It is a dyadic, asymmetrical relationship in which individuals exchange something valued, to their perceived mutual advantage. The individuals need not be equal in resources; indeed, the patron has control of far greater resources than the client. But the client brings to the patron something that the latter needs, such as deference, material goods, votes, or other forms of support; in return the patron supplies him with something desired, such as a job, political access, or protection. The patron may in turn be the client of a more influential patron, who may in turn be a client, and so on. The chain can stretch from the very lowest to the very highest level of the system, though in Tarrow's words, it "lengthens obligation beyond the scope of effective political allocation."[17] Tarrow writes that "an individual is linked to the authority structure through personal ties of obligation and loyalty, rather than through the merger of his interests with others of the same social group or ideological persuasion. Hence, politics is nonideological, broad functional interests cannot be expressed in politics, and access to authority can expand only through the further vertical extension of clientele links."[18] Ties are person to person, face to face, and this is true even of formally bureaucratic organizations. The state is a bureaucratic entity represented by the police, the courts, the tax collector; it penetrates the society through a network of local relationships that intervenes between citizen and state so that even bureaucratic functions are infused with local and personalistic concerns.

Zuckerman has pointed out the differing implications of cliental and social class analyses of the formation of political groups.[19] The latter assumes that people with similar locations in the social stratification system will form political groups with one another. Under clientelism people with similar locations will form political groups with others at different locations, because they perceive their interests to conflict with those of others at similar locations.[20] As a result, one competes with those most similar and cooperates with those higher and lower in the stratification system. This has immense implications for collective action.

It is obvious that the patron-client tie involves a form of representation, and also that it is quite different in its consequences from other forms.[21] Clientelism seems particularly adapted to a parochial society in which collective action is restrained, levels of political competence are low, and the absence of extensive economic change renders life a zero-sum game. In such a society, Banfield's "amoral familism"— "maximize the material, short-run advantage of the nuclear family; assume that all others will do likewise"—may not be irrational at all.[22] What is important for our discussion of representation is that it is face to face, individualistic, elite dominated, and, we would argue, oriented toward the perpetuation of the status quo even when it permits considerable individual mobility. Like other forms of representation, it too can become institutionalized in legislatures and develop great endurance.[23] In fact, one of the changes that students of patron-client relationships have noted in diverse locales is the rise of institutional patrons such as the political party. This has certainly been the case in Italy, where parties often function as institutionalized patrons and where patron-client linkages are important in the electoral process and especially so in the policy process.

This discussion of clientelism suggests that notions of representation that have grown out of the Anglo-American tradition may be ill suited for the analysis of many systems.[24] Another example will reinforce that view. If only a small segment of the elite is mobilized, it may be normatively correct to say that the system is unrepresentative. But understanding is not advanced very much thereby, for representation acquires significance only with mobilization. And in the absence of nonelectoral forms of mobilization, attempts to alter a system through free elections are not likely to make it more truly representative. Mobilization is related to the organizational complexity of the polity. It is possible for political organization to substitute for other forms of organizational development, but this seems to work only in special circumstances in which existing elites are unable for various reasons to prevent the growth of rival political organizations. In most circumstances existing elites can frustrate political efforts and manipulate elections if the organizational base for mass mobilization is not present.

With increases in organizational complexity and expansion of political competence on the part of both masses and potential counterelites, there is a corresponding increase in the potential for mass mobilization. We emphasize the word potential, for there are many strategies for limiting and delaying the growth of mass mobilization; hence high levels of complexity and competence are necessary but not sufficient conditions for it. As mass mobilization proceeds, it becomes increasingly difficult for elites to deny representation in decision making to new groups. With mobilization the effective polity expands to include more and more people. Today the polity includes everyone at least symbolically, in the sense that only complete universal suffrage seems to be normatively acceptable in the twentieth century, though in fact in all polities there are social groups that have no real influence on decision making. This process of incorporating new groups may proceed smoothly, or it may involve violence and discontinuities in the political system.[25] Why one or the other results in a particular country is an often researched question, but general answers remain unsatisfactory and inadequate.

In Western liberal democracies mass mobilization has led to the formal representation of the mobilized groups in legislatures. This is not the same thing as representation in policymaking. The relationship between the two varies from country to country. Other aspects of representation may be of equal importance in their consequences. For example, one very important by-product of formal representation is the disciplining of mobilized groups. In some systems, formal representation via the electoral game has institutionalized dissent without really involving the newly mobilized groups in the policy process. We believe that this was for a long time a consequence of the Communist and Socialist mobilization of certain groups in Italy, though the degree of actual influence of these groups on policymaking is the subject of debate and disagreement.

With political power comes the ability to influence and often to determine which lines of cleavage in society will be represented. It is comparable on the structural level to agenda setting on the decision-making level. Thus if Marxist parties could make social class the predominant line of cleavage they would perhaps win all elections. But religious-secular, interconfessional, center-periphery, linguistic, cultural, ideological, and many other lines of cleavage continue to intrude on politics. And the persistence of organizations insures that once cleavages get institutionalized in parties and other organizations they are likely to continue for a long time to influence politics even if, from many points of view, they seem outmoded. While systems may not really be "frozen," as Lipset and Rokkan suggest, their very institutionalization channels politics into particular lines of cleavage, encourages some paths of evolution and not others, and extends the legacy of history into unpredictable corners of politics.[26] Consequently, what the "real" lines of cleavage are in a society is ultimately a political issue. Like other political issues, its outcome depends upon the historical context, the skills and goals of politicians, and, probably to a greater extent than we wish to recognize, random events. This latter insures that national variations will be considerable and that general theory will be developed only with difficulty.

ON REPRESENTATION AND THE STUDY OF LEGISLATURES

Scholarly concern with representation has grown out of the study of legislatures and legislators, and several aspects of the present design reflect this particular research tradition.[27] As Loewenberg has pointed out, "The academic study of legislatures has long been influenced by an eighteenth-century model of the political system, a model which regards the legislature as the central policy-making institution that Anglo-American constitutional lawyers in the seventeenth and eighteenth centuries expected it to be. This is a demand-input model of representative institutions which assumes that citizens have well-formulated policy preferences and that the function of the members of the representative assembly is to convert these preferences into public policies."[28] The debate has not strayed far from the format established by Edmund Burke in the argument over whether the representative was a trustee or a delegate. Empirical work has demonstrated that mass publics are poorly informed about what their representatives do and that issues are only one variable—one whose importance can vary a great deal—in the electoral decision. But research has also shown that information levels are often high and voting patterns discriminating on those issues that have high saliency for voters.[29]

In Italy we are faced with a situation in which information levels are low, in which there is great consistency in voting despite the brief history of the current political regime, and in which parties intervene between the represented and the representative. The demand-input model is thus inadequate; we must alter our focus.

Sartori has distinguished the three functions of legislatures as representation, legislation, and control of the administration.[30] We focus on the first, with little attention to the others. We develop what Eulau and Hinckley call the "outside" rather than the "inside" model of legislative behavior.[31] That is, we examine the relationships between the legislator's behavior and influences outside the legislature such as constituency, party, background, and beliefs; we are not concerned with the decision-making process inside the legislature or with legislative-executive relationships.[32]

The outside model has been especially suited to the republican era in Italy, because of the nature of the fit between the process of representation and the decision-making process at the national level. This fit varies greatly from one country to another, but republican Italy undoubtedly has ranked high among its peers in the relative independence of electoral inputs and policy outputs.[33] Inputs and outputs involved different processes, different games, that intersected rarely and irregularly. The electoral game involved a large number of players; it was open, democratic, and largely free of corruption.[34] It had an impact on long-range trends in policymaking because it affected the nature of the coalition and perceptions of the future, but for long periods during the republican era elections led to few changes in specific policies and programs. The electoral game was open, at least to the major players; the policymaking game on the national level was largely restricted to players who had been close to the dominant party in the electoral game, augmented by individuals, groups, and institutions that carried societal weight and whose interests did not clash with or greatly threaten those of the dominant party.[35] Thus the second largest party, the Italian Communist Party (PCI), was left almost completely out of the formal policymaking game on the national level; the business community, on the other hand, which in part supported the Italian Liberal party (PLI) as well as the Christian Democratic (DC) and other parties in electoral politics, had ready access to the dominant party in the policy game.

The system that had operated to insulate the policy game from the electoral game in the postwar period was beginning to crack at the time of this study; the growing electoral strength of the Communists increasingly reduced DC dominance. In the absence of a clear majority, the DC had to secure parliamentary support from other parties, either through coalition or through support for cabinets and policies on an ad hoc basis. These one-party cabinets—*monocolore* or "single color" governments—existed through the votes or abstinence of allies that had no cabinet positions. A heritage of de Gaspari's leadership was a DC preference for coalition partners even when not absolutely necessary. And with the "Opening to the Left" in the 1960s, the coalition widened to include the Italian Socialist party (PSI), which had previously been part of the left opposition. PSI support was bought at some cost, for the DC had to implement several reforms. Beginning in 1960 the PSI supported but did not enter the new majority; in late 1963 the

PSI accepted cabinet positions in a new coalition. It later entered into an incomplete merger with the PSDI, the Social Democratic party.

It was the very convincing argument of the electoral returns that led to the Opening to the Left, demonstrating that elections did have a long-term impact. One of the chief results of PSI support was its inclusion in the policy game, from which the left had generally been excluded.

This expansion of the majority to include the Socialists as well as the Social Democrats and Republicans created great problems for the dominant DC. A badly fragmented party held together by religion and the fruits of power, the DC was a precarious union of religious, industrial, agricultural, and trade-union interests that coexisted uneasily. The lack of coherence within the party rendered unified decision making difficult, with the result that DC politicians had to mediate among competing interests and seldom were able to provide effective leadership in developing unified and general programs for meeting national needs. The difficulty of achieving formal agreement and action encouraged informal, and often illegal, patterns of influence, patronage, and accommodation referred to as the *sottogoverno* ("undergovernment," as in "underworld").[36] Neither parliament nor the cabinet itself had much control over individual ministries. The most important routes of access to decision makers were informal, through contacts with influential party and bureaucratic officials.[37] These in turn used their offices to further their individual career interests. The policy process thus involved the personal aspirations and friendships of the key decision makers as much as it did the open play of political forces in parliament.

The Socialists became deeply involved in this *sottogoverno*, with individual ministries and state enterprises becoming Socialist fiefdoms. A result was internal fighting in the PSI over these spoils, as well as a deeper struggle for the soul of the party. The Socialists were increasingly compromised by their role in the policy game, and the Communists reaped the electoral benefits of widespread public disgust.

General disillusionment was intensified by the nature of coalition making in Italy. The major programs of government emerged from the internal struggle within the governing DC, plus the bargaining process between that party and other parties that made up the coalition. The coalition agreement raised great hopes that seemed always to be frustrated by the inability of the coalition to enact more than a portion of what had been promised. Seemingly, programs should have been enacted without difficulty, since they had governmental majorities behind them. However, there was seldom agreement on details, and parliament provided the opportunity for sabotage by groups within the coalition. As the important votes could be secret, it was possible for members of parliament who should have been supporting the program because of party discipline to vote against it almost with impunity. These *franchi tiratori*, or snipers, caused the failure of programs and "shot down" several cabinets.

It is difficult to evaluate the parliamentary role of the opposition.[38] There is evidence that it worked quite effectively and cooperatively in committees. But much parliamentary and committee activity was of limited importance. Parliamentary debate was addressed as much to public opinion, especially that of a party's own followers, as to the specific legislation under discussion. Even when dealing with genuine decisions that affected the policy process, parliament was also playing the electoral game, in which actions were determined by their impact upon party strategies in that contest rather than upon policymaking. Of course, this is not unique to the Italian political system; all legislators are concerned with the electoral consequences of what they do. But the fit between the electoral and policy games was especially poor in Italy during most of the postwar period; much of what went on in the legislature had little impact on policymaking. In terms of Sartori's typology of legislative functions, parliament played a limited role in the actual, as opposed to the formal, process of lawmaking and almost no role in control of the administration.

Parliament was poorly equipped to do more. Staff was minimal, access to needed information extremely limited, the administration uncooperative, and the coherence of parliament as an institution poorly developed. Parliamentarians relied heavily on their parties' organizations for direction and information.[39] Most legislative research was carried out by the staff of the parties and not by parliamentary employees. In some parties, extraparliamentary institutions, especially the party organization, sometimes seemed to overshadow the work of parliament.

Thus the outside model appears to be the more promising as a focus for the study of representation in Italy. From the viewpoint of representation, what went on in parliament was not nearly as important as what went on among the parties and the electorate, organized interests, and the administration. Following up on the suggestions of Eulau and Prewitt concerning linkages, we believe that representation takes place in any linkage that involves political elites being responsive to the preferences of the public or some part of it.[40] A thorough study of representation would therefore have to include inquiries into all aspects of these linkages and hence would have to examine both the policy and the electoral processes. But as we have begun with more conventional assumptions concerning representation, we have concentrated on the electoral process. It is our belief that in Italy at the time of our fieldwork elite-mass congruence was greater in that process than in the policy process. Individual elections had little impact on altering the composition of the government: The Christian Democratic party held the majority of ministries and most of the important ministries, including the presidency of the council of ministers (office of the prime minister), from 1946 until the time of writing thirty years later.

Perhaps Italy represents in extreme form what Loewenberg has suggested is the major difference between the American and European traditions in the functioning of the legislature. He argues that in the European tradition its principal function is consensus building rather than lawmaking, as the latter is an executive-administration function that is shared only marginally with parliament. [41] The Italian system is certainly closer to the European than to the American model, but it does not fit either one very well. [42]

Galli and Prandi explain the Italian situation somewhat differently: While Communists and Catholics both participate in parliament, they do not entirely accept the spirit of its constitutional design. [43] Neither Catholics nor Communists, for instance, share the classical view of political representation as enacting the purely political will of discrete sovereign units—the individual citizens. Although Catholics and Communists disagree on which of the individual's multiple social memberships is of ultimate significance in determining his political interests, both view the individual not simply as a "citizen," but rather as a member of a social category. They tend to view parliament not as the locus of political decisions based on majority agreement among individual representatives, but as a mirror of social forces that, though they arise outside of parliament, seek a legal sanction there. These extraparliamentary forces are crucial in the study of representation in Italy.

THE PRESENT STUDY

The present study focuses on representatives, their constituents, and the institutions that mediate the linkage between them. It is one of a series of studies carried out by scholars at the Center for Political Studies, Institute for Social Research of The University of Michigan, on a Ford Foundation institutional grant. The series expands the theoretical concerns first operationalized by Miller and Stokes in their classic study of American congressional-constituency linkages. [44] The general outline of our research reflects their design, with some particularly Italian variations. We have interviewed a national mass sample and a sample of deputies. The most important of our alterations stem from the consequences of the Italian system of proportional representation and the strong role of the party. The multimember districts and the system of preference voting caused us to decide not to interview defeated candidates. The fact that the most important votes in parliament are secret made the investigation of roll-call votes seem a poor investment of resources. Finally, because of the importance of party we wished to understand more about its functioning at lower levels, so we have interviewed a sample of communal councillors, who are elected local representatives. Both the deputies and councillors were selected from the Italian Communist Party, the Italian Socialist Party-Italian Social Democratic Party, and the Christian Democratic Party. In 1968, these three parties together received 81.5 percent of the national vote for the Chamber of Deputies and 84.6 percent of the seats in that body. Details of the research design are found in the Appendix.

This study treats several aspects of Italian political behavior that may on first reading seem only tangentially related to the problem of representation as it has been conventionally operationalized. There are two reasons for this. The first and theoretically compelling one is that our view of representation as the normative dimension of mobilization requires us to examine aspects of behavior that go beyond issues of congruence on policy preferences and opinions. Hence we look at many aspects of people's involvement in politics, and we pay particular attention to the role of the party and other mediating institutions. The second reason for the detailed treatment of several aspects of behavior is that less is known about political behavior in Italy than is the case for several other countries, especially the United States. As a consequence we include analyses that would not be necessary in a study of representation in many other countries.

We do not claim to have presented a new theory of representation in this chapter. We have presented a perspective, and that is a beginning. We are concerned with the implications for theory of our findings about Italy. This study is a contribution to a common enterprise—the construction of general empirical statements about representation—and it is also a study of a single country. This dual purpose is evident throughout. The next chapter focuses on the specifically Italian aspects of the perspective sketched out above.

2

The Parties and the
Institutionalization of Tradition

If by institutions we mean "stable, valued, recurring patterns of behavior," the Italian republic is a highly institutionalized polity with few
equals among contemporary states.[1] Among these institutions there
are many that would be conceded to be primarily political and governmental, though there are many that are not, as is true of all polities.
And much that is unique in Italian politics stems from the political
importance of institutions that are nongovernmental and in some cases
not even primarily political.

At the societal level the single most important Italian institution is
undoubtedly the Catholic church.[2] By most standards and definitions it
would be considered the institution that personifies one end of any
continuum of institutionalization.[3] The Church is of course involved in
politics, but it is much more than what is generally meant by a political
institution. Many other major societal institutions are political yet also
much more, such as cooperatives, farm organizations, trade unions,
and even the political parties.[4]

These institutions intervene between the citizen and the structures
of government, so that loyalty to the latter is mediated by nongovernmental institutions. As a result, the legitimacy that in many
other systems—and especially those that have been the focus of much
research on representation—is vested in the agencies of government,
such as the legislature, executive, and judiciary, throughout much of
the republican era was granted in Italy to the Church, the political
parties, and their associated organizations. That these institutions

17

stood between the individual and the government had important consequences for loyalties as well as legitimacy, for it rendered individual attachment to the political system conditional on the continued loyalties of the institutions, and especially their elites, to the system. With the maturation of postwar generations that were socialized under republican institutions, these loyalties are likely to be focused increasingly on the governmental institutions themselves. But at the time of the study, in 1968, this shift was not yet clearly evident at the mass level.

The limited legitimacy of governmental institutions undoubtedly contributed to the generally low score of Italians on measures of affect for the political system. They also scored high on alienation, and they exhibited less trust in authorities and regime.[5] More positive consequences were an absence of national chauvinism, a distrust of concentrated power, a high level of toleration in practice even when not justified by ideology, and an equally high level of political realism that easily slid into cynicism.

Daalder has raised the question of the compatibility of "loyalties to subcultural groups and the state."[6] This is an important but neglected consideration for some types of pluralist systems. An obvious consequence in Italy is that subcultural loyalties strengthen the role of elites in the system, since it is primarily they who determine the stance of the subcultural groups toward the system. These mediating structures and their elites thus assume paramount importance.

Huntington has described institutionalization as "the process by which organizations and procedures acquire value and stability. The level of institutionalization of any political system can be defined by the adaptability, complexity, autonomy, and coherence of its organizations and procedures."[7] If we apply these criteria to the Italian political system as a whole, the parties, Church, and other related organizations meet them quite well. That is, Italian politics is strongly institutionalized if we think of the traditions as the units that are involved.

The traditions to which we refer are sets of expectations about life in general that are held by large numbers of people, expectations that are transmitted through the family, formal organizations, and numerous informal ways. Although the traditions have political consequences, they relate to other dimensions of life as well. Although they have ideologies associated with them, they involve far more than the cognitive dimension. Although they are concentrated in particular subcultures, the fit between subculture and tradition is poor, because some subcultures contain several traditions and the traditions spread across several subcultures. Although they are given societal expression through organizations, they involve much more than is evident in their institutional manifestations alone. With all of the risks attendant on using a familiar word in an unfamiliar manner, we find the concept of tradition necessary to specify what is represented in Italy. The basic cleavage is between traditions. Tradition is not just ideology, or subculture, or organization; it is all of these. It is the traditions that bind together the disparate elements and give cohesion to Italian politics.

The central role of traditions in the process of representation is not unique to Italy. Several countries exhibit similar patterns of the interplay of history, ideology, interests, subcultures, and organization; and in these countries the institutionalization of tradition has likewise made great headway. We refer to what has been labeled "consociational democracy,"[8] "segmented pluralism,"[9] "amicable agreement,"[10] and *proporzdemokratie*.[11] The polities that reflect these patterns in their purest form are said to be the Netherlands, Austria, Switzerland, and Belgium; Lebanon before 1975 and Canada are also sometimes viewed as approximating them.[12] The chief political consequence of consociational democracy, as it is most commonly called, is the sharing of state power among the traditions. Each mobilizes its partisans thoroughly in organizations rigidly separate from the other traditions. Elites bargain on behalf of their traditions; the public policy that emerges is the result of this process of compromise, with elites having virtual veto power over proposals that they view as threatening to the core values of their traditions. Such a system evolves when partisan elites acknowledge that no single tradition can dominate and that all must thus come to terms in order to avoid chaos and stalemate.

Italy was most definitely not a consociational democracy at the time of the fieldwork in 1968 or of writing in 1976. It was a dominant party system; there was no genuine sharing of power. Furthermore, neither the DC nor the PCI exhibited the openness, trust, restraint, and pragmatism common to consociational democracies. It was possible that the "Historic Compromise" advocated by the PCI would inaugurate such a system. Several observers considered it an alternative path for the evolution of the system.[13] But during the period that we examine such possibilities seemed far in the future. Italian traditions appeared to be more pervasive, deeply rooted, and inflexible than those of functioning consociational democracies. Moreover, no consociational democracy had a strong Communist party, and though all of those mentioned had important religious parties, none is the home of the Vatican. Finally, Italian political elites seemed to lack the freedom of action in bargaining possessed by the elites of consociational democracies.

Italian parties, as organizations, lack autonomy from the traditions for which they are the electoral vehicles. This is especially evident in the Christian Democratic party, which is heavily dependent on institutions that are less specifically political. The organizational structures of the left, on the other hand, are much more explicitly political; but some, such as unions and cooperatives, are not primarily oriented toward electoral politics and consequently complicate the political strategies of their traditions.

If some of the parties lack autonomy, the institutions of government are even less autonomous. Compare, for example, the Italian parliament with the United States House of Representatives as analyzed by Polsby, who notes as characteristics of an institutionalized organization that it is well bounded and differentiated from its environment; complex; and universalistic and automatic, rather than particularistic and discretionary, in its methods.[14] There is no doubt that by this definition the House is far more institutionalized than the Italian Chamber of Deputies. And there is also little doubt that primary loyalties in Italy have in the past attached more to the traditions and their institutional manifestations than to the Chamber and other governmental institutions.

This fact has important consequences for the stability of the political system. In some respects, the Italian system is extremely stable. Focusing on its frequent turnover of governments and its limited problem-solving capacity ignores the long domination of the Christian Democratic party and the remarkable continuity in Italian voting patterns that has been documented by several studies.[15]

It seems that in the past loyalties were to the traditions and not to the constitutional system, hence deeper system stability and even survival were often called into question. For if party elites were to decide that the present constitutional order was not acceptable and should be replaced, it was uncertain that many citizens would place loyalty to the system ahead of loyalty to party and tradition. Yet, while the constitutional system did not meet the expectations and preferences of all of the parties, it was the system that was least objectionable to most of them. That is, except for the extremes on the right and left, the constitutional order enjoyed widespread support among all major parties, including the constitutional right and the Communist left. It was the system that divided Italy least. But, for example, if the Communist leaders were to opt for altering it, most Communist voters might very well follow them, and if the Church authorities were to determine that a good Catholic could no longer support the regime or the constitutional order, a majority of the Christian Democratic following and much of that of the right might likewise go along with the change. Of course, the particular circumstances under which these elite choices were exercised would make a big difference in the responses of Communist and Catholic voters. Elite attitudes are crucial, and it is very important that even in 1968 few parliamentarians seemed to favor substantial change: Putnam found that few of the deputies in his sample "expressed any desire to abolish the institutions of the Republic or even to modify them in any fundamental way."[16] Our deputy interviews reveal similar sentiments.

Yet, during much of the republican period, the constitutional order seemed less important than the traditions. Governmental institutions lacked autonomy. Legitimacy was mediated by the parties and the traditions. Mass commitment to the constitutional order was fragile. This is not a forecast of the future; we do not claim that it will always be so. Institutionalization takes a long time. The Church and the parties were older than the Italian constitutional order; with time, the latter seemed to be assuming primacy. We are talking about a particular historical period, and there seems little doubt concerning the crucial role of the mediating structures during that time.

THE ITALIAN TRADITIONS

Italy is fragmented along several lines of cleavage—including ideological, subcultural, social class, regional, and organizational dimensions— and any attempt to demonstrate that any single one of these is the dominant cleavage is doomed to failure. Cleavages combine in different ways in each of the political groupings; each thus reflects unique sets of dimensions, which we call traditions. They are patterns of thinking and acting that originated in concrete historical situations, have become institutionalized, and are perpetuated in various ways. Italian traditions are not primarily political as are, for example, the Democratic and Republican "traditions" in the United States; unlike the *familles politiques* of France, they are more than ideologies and tendencies.[17] Finally, unlike political parties in many countries, they are not merely organizations primarily pursuing public office. Yet, as we have said, they are all of these things.

The traditions continue to exist long after the passage of the historical period that gave them birth. This is the dark side of institutionaliza-

21

tion: It perpetuates past divisions. Parties follow the general tendency of organisms to survive; several traditions and parties exist today mainly because they existed in the past and possess an organization rather than because of their functional significance. If they did not exist it would not be necessary to found them. Each of these regimes that dominated Italy left a residue, not only in historical memory—which is a not unimportant thing—but also in societal institutions and in the structure of the representation of interests. In the absence of revolutionary destruction of the social bases of political groups, there has been a growing complexity of Italian political traditions: None dies and few decline. The tradition survives, and the party along with it, as long as its social base retains the vitality to preserve it.

The perpetuation of parties and traditions has been remarkable despite the massive transformations that have swept Italy since the Second World War. An important reason is that close ties exist between traditions and access to political influence in a political system that seldom employs universalistic criteria in dispensing its favors. This encourages a tendency to hang on to what one has and to avoid experimentation with alternative forms of organization and behavior. The rewards for innovation in Italian politics in the past have not been very great.

Institutionalization permits dissatisfaction to be contained within the tradition. Dissidents need not leave; they can work within the tradition, hence dissatisfaction encourages renewal rather than disaffection. The major traditions contain dissenters, especially among the young; all have had to deal with threats and sometimes the reality of schism. Yet historically, much accommodation with dissent has been possible.

Until this point we have spoken about the traditions in quite general terms. Now we will begin to be more specific. Although the traditions have substantive content, a great deal of disagreement can exist over what particular typology of traditions is the most useful. For example, a fundamental distinction exists in Italy between left and right. For some purposes it would be useful and proper to refer to these as the two basic Italian traditions. Left and right do have considerable discriminatory power; they are useful for some purposes but not for others. These two broad political groupings are subdivided into different and often competing traditions, and it is past successes that have determined which tradition is on the left and which on the right.

Following Mannheim, Lasswell and Kaplan provide, in their distinction between ideology and utopia, a useful analytical tool for beginning our discussion of the relationship between left and right and the tradi-

22

tions. "The *ideology* is the political myth functioning to preserve the social structure; the *utopia*, to supplant it."[18] Each regime that has ruled Italy has had an ideology; each ideology thus has had a social location in particular social groups; particular social groups maintain the tradition, and along with it the ideology, party, subculture, and patterns of interest articulation that served it best, which usually resemble the forms of the regime under which it was dominant. The fit is not perfect, for some social groups prospered under more than one regime, and these groups today are likely to divide their political loyalties among several traditions. The converse is equally true: Some traditions, such as the Catholic, have prospered under several regimes, though not equally, and in this case the tradition is likely to contain several partial ideologies and preferences for institutional forms that coexist uneasily together.

Past regimes have left residues in the form of traditions and ideologies; their oppositions have left residues in the form of traditions and utopias. These utopias have through time themselves become institutionalized, though they have never dominated at the national level; and it is essentially this distinction between present and former establishments and their oppositions, rather than conventional socioeconomic dimensions, that separates right and left in Italy.

The terms "left" and "right" are widely employed by elites and masses in Italy. But while the terms may themselves inspire loyalties and fervent devotion in some countries, in Italy such attachments are reserved for more concrete entities. Indeed, the existence of strong loyalties to particular traditions rather than to the left and right in general leads to competition within those two categories that is often as severe as that between them. Thus we must move from left and right categories to more specific traditions and then in an even more precise manner to the parties and other organizations that are the institutional foci of loyalties.

Although there is debate concerning the nuances and fringes of Italian traditions, there is substantial agreement concerning their main outlines.[19] Bellah accepts Croce's labels of what the latter called "opposing religious faiths."[20] These are liberalism, Catholicism, socialism, and what Croce, utilizing a certain prudence writing under Fascism, called "activism," which included Fascism as well as other varieties. Bellah adds "prechristian" or "subchristian" to this list.[21] While Croce viewed these in a static fashion, Gramsci arrived at a dynamic, Marxist interpretation of a progression of what he preferred to call "ideologies," or simply "politics."[22] These dominated the Italian scene one after the other. Our position is that these two points of view are easily reconciled, for if we take a slice of reality and study a particular moment in time, as we have done in our 1968 representation study, all of these traditions are very much in evidence (including Bellah's "prechristian"). If we take a dynamic view, the perspective is modified, as some of them seem to be in the ascendancy and some in decline.

In our opinion the institutionalization of these traditions has facilitated their survival. Only a thoroughgoing restructuring of society could eradicate them. For example, it is conceivable that the liberal could be wiped out, and perhaps the activist, too, since it depends almost as much on the party as on other societal organizations such as the bureaucracy for a base. But it is not credible to expect any regime to wipe out the Catholic church and its institutional structure. More feasible would be an accommodation between it and its competitors. This has happened in the past, leaving the Church intact and often purified. For the Catholic tradition in Italy has historically attracted opportunists who embrace it for the political rewards that it can dispense.[23] Its deep roots, its hierarchical structure, its experience in survival have all made it a pole of attraction for those seeking to preserve any particular status quo. Adversity and attack might reduce the number of its formal adherents but would probably strengthen its internal cohesion. After two millenia of adaptation—a prime characteristic of an institution—it would be unwise to expect its imminent disintegration.

The prechristian—Bellah's own addition to the list enumerated by Croce—merits clarification. He is referring to beliefs and practices handed down from generation to generation, practices that emphasize trusting only intimates and being loyal only to face-to-face groups rather than abstractions such as class or nation.[24] This prechristian religion undergirds the other traditions, reinforcing clientelism and the particularism of what we have called the policy game. It is not a separate tradition so much as it is a deeply ingrained set of assumptions and practices that has a profound impact on all the traditions, though more on some than on others. Thus clientelism was more important a century ago than it is today, and it is more important in some parts of the country than in others; but like the other traditions it is deeply institutionalized. Although it may be in decline relative to the others, it is unlikely to disappear completely in the near future and should be viewed as a seldom acknowledged but ubiquitous component of all Italian traditions.

The institutionalization of these traditions must be seen in the historical context of the mobilization of the population. The liberal tradition dominated the unification of Italy. The extension of the suffrage and mutual antipathy led to the simultaneous expansion of the Catholic and socialist traditions, which were in opposition to the liberals. The activist tradition has been in part a cover for status-quo-oriented groups and in part a form of escapism for the young and the romantic. Traditions of the right are those that have dominated Italy in the past and hence as a consequence have penetrated central societal institutions. The left has never been dominant on the national scene, but it is likewise increasingly institutionalized in various ways, having created countercultural institutions as well as dominating governmental structures at the subnational levels. Left parties historically have drifted toward accommodation with the status quo; hence, the older the left party, the more rightist it is. The Italian Republican party (PRI), for example, emerged from the nineteenth-century opposition to both the monarchical and Catholic traditions. Its residue today is concentrated in the geographical areas and social groups that opposed the manner in which unification was achieved and that maintained hostility toward both the monarchy and the Church. This was a period of limited suffrage and elite rule, and the contemporary opposition was itself part of the elite.

The socialist parties, on the other hand, first prospered in the period of mass mobilization. The Marxist ideology, or utopia, provided the intellectual foundations of a mass movement based on trade unions, cooperatives, Chambers of Labor, and other working-class organizations; this movement converted an emerging proletariat, and in some areas an awakening peasantry as well, into a reasonably well-integrated counterculture. The ideology did not create the counterculture; neither did the organizations. The counterculture was as much the result of the pattern of national integration and of industrial development as of ideology or of organization. But the socialists mobilized the counterculture and created a separate tradition out of part of it. Ideology provides a cognitive appeal that has been crucial in supplying the tradition with intellectuals, which is very important in a society that values intellectual debate highly. Thus the different aspects of the tradition can attract intellectuals, organized interests, and the socially marginal; yet the tradition itself is not to be identified completely with any of these sources of support.

The socialist tradition has undergone considerable transformation through time, and there has been a continual struggle over which organizational structure would speak for it. In the early years of the century there were competing socialist organizations, joined by the Communists after the Bolshevik revolution. After the fall of fascism, the Communists became the dominant organizational form within the left. Their victory was not complete, however, for both ideology and interests provided a basis for other organizations with which the Communists have had to share the left tradition.

The strength of these organizations of the left is related to their utopianism. That is, the older strands have moved close to power, to accommodation with the ruling regimes, and they either never had or they have lost much of their mass following in the process. Thus the Republicans are the oldest of the left parties; they were also in 1968 the closest to power, the smallest in electoral strength, and the highest in the status of their membership and electorate. The two socialist parties are next in age. The Social Democrats have been closer to the ruling Christian Democratic party; indeed, some observers refuse to consider them to be on the left at all, because of their generally conservative role in the coalition process as well as their anticommunism. We treat them as of the left because that is how they are perceived by both elites and masses in our samples. The PSI did not cooperate closely with the Christian Democrats until the years of the Opening to the Left when the two socialist parties merged; moreover, the PSI sought to keep communications open with the Communists. The Social Democrats received fewer votes than the Socialists but more than the Republicans. The Communists are of course the largest of all and, in our sense of the term, the most utopian of the major left parties. While the extraparliamentary leftist groups are even more utopian, they lack the minimal level of systemic accommodation necessary to compete seriously in the electoral game; as a consequence they are not a force from the point of view of parliamentary representation, though they are of interest for other reasons. The Republicans, Social Democrats, Socialists, and Communists form a continuum in terms of electoral strength, age, closeness to power, utopianism, and social status of their memberships and electorates.

Why does this continuum exist? Certainly the nature of the mobilization patterns at the time of the party's initial successes is important, with each new revitalization of the left requiring innovative and more complex techniques for mobilizing segments of the population never fully involved before. A handicap of new parties today is that almost the entire population is now closely aligned with the existing parties. New movements must not only attract the uncommitted; they must also break the ties that bind the electorate to the present parties. In a sense, they must disaffiliate before they can mobilize. Hence they have been most successful with the young, who have not developed strong commitments. The success of the Communists in mobilizing the left, combined with the high rate of voting turnout, thus served to stabilize the electorate. One could almost say that it disciplined the electorate: Successful incorporation of the mass of voters into the existing patterns of power, including the institutionalization of opposition, resulted in great electoral stability. It also probably eliminated most of the potential for great revolutionary change from the Italian political system.

Three final observations are in order concerning the evolution of the traditions. First, change has taken place mainly through the marginal advantages of one party or another from one election to another rather than through dramatic shifts either in preferences or behaviors of the electorate. Second, the marginal changes are cumulative in the sense that they seem to reflect patterns of mobilization and population replacement rather than responses to topical issues. Third, throughout most of the republican era, the greatest changes were between parties within the ideological and within the utopian—the right and left— segments of the electorate rather than between them. Although changes were small, some flexibility accrued to the system from their exploitation by party elites to alter the orientation of their parties. That is, in the constant search for marginal advantage in the coalition games—both the governmental and electoral coalition games, which are different—factional leaders used shifting electoral fortunes to advance their own positions within the parties and their parties within the political spectrum.

THE EVOLUTION OF THE PARTIES

Italian unity was achieved by secularly oriented elites who were disproportionately distributed over the country.[25] Although unification had support in all regions, it was the north that dominated. These new national elites came to terms with traditional and subnational elites in a highly selective fashion, often granting them a free hand locally in return for support or acquiescence in national policies of centralization and modernization, policies that were extremely uneven in their impact on different regions of the country. The national elites were in general liberal in economics and often in philosophical outlook as well. They supported the monarchy as a source of stability and conservatism.

In the process of unification, the Church lost its secular territories, and only in the Lateran treaties under the Fascists were the rights of the Church within unified Italy and papal control over the Vatican City itself formalized. This struggle, combined with the philosophical stance of the leaders of the new Italy, caused the Church to oppose unification; Catholics were forbidden to participate in the affairs of the new state that had been formed in part at the expense of the papacy, and the new regime was deprived of the active support of an important segment of the population. This does not mean that practicing Catholics necessarily opposed unification and political involvement, but papal intransigence hindered their participation greatly. Nevertheless, Catholic involvement gradually increased, and they finally formed the Popular party, which won the second highest number of votes and seats in the election of 1919. Before then, Catholics had been electorally active in support of conservative candidates.

The political system established following unification was elite dominated, with property requirements for voting and a small electorate. The Catholic masses were unmobilized; the emerging urban proletariat, denied the vote and attracted by anarchism, was not an important political force until late in the century after the formation and growth of the labor movement and the Socialist party. In the absence of Catholic and leftist participation, the system was dominated by the liberal elite and a small and unstable group of radicals, some of whom represented the present Republican tradition in opposition to both the monarchy and the Church.

As more and more people were able to meet the requirements for voting, the elitist system was threatened by the growth of the left. The incorporation of the Catholic masses into the system as a conservative force was a way to counterbalance the rising Socialist party. But the liberal politicians themselves were unable to absorb these new groups of voters into their system of mutual favoritism. The result was a long-term decline in the electoral strength of the notables and the rise of two mass movements, one Socialist and one Catholic. Their rise, however, did not eliminate personalistic politics, in which local notables construct a network of followers through mutual favoritism, pork-barrel politics, and intimidation. The nineteenth-century party system relied almost exclusively on these practices, to the neglect of party organization and ideology; clientelism still retains considerable importance, especially as a source of preference votes, and in some areas of the south substantial electoral shifts sometimes signify that the local patron has changed his party rather than that any change has taken place in the opinions of the electorate. The Neofascists, Christian Democrats, Liberals, and Monarchists rely heavily on these methods, especially in the south, and clientelism is an important element in all parties, including those of the left, in that region.

Clientelistic patterns were the dominant form of mobilization in the nineteenth century; it was not until the rise of the left that parties as organizations acquired great significance in Italy. The nineteenth-century elites were notables who tended their own fences with the assistance on a personal basis of the prime minister and prefect. Cabinets were formed on the basis of these personal arrangements (*trasformismo*) with few considerations of ideology or party organizational needs. It was a system that functioned well only with a restricted electorate. The rise of the left and later of the Popular party left the notables without a mass following. This electoral weakness added to the attractions of Fascism for the traditional political elites of the country, which in turn contributed to the discrediting of many of them at the end of the Second World War.

In fact, under Fascism the polity was administered by a specialized political elite using organizational forms better adapted to an age of mass mobilization, while the traditional elites continued to dominate the economy and society.[26] Because it capitalized on a pre-existing layer of dispositions, Fascism was able to simulate being a mass movement with a popular base, though there is little evidence that it made much of an impact at the mass level.[27] But it did provide the means for controlling mass publics in an age in which traditional forms of exclusion and repression were losing their effectiveness.

Organski has interpreted Italian Fascism as a syncratic polity, one based on the sharing of rule by the industrial and agricultural elites.[28] It arose at a time when neither was able to dominate the other, and in which both were threatened by the mobilization of the urban and rural masses. It dominated the polity for twenty years, and some elites retain evidence to the present day of their socialization under it. This is especially true of the group that probably wielded greatest power under that regime relative to others—the bureaucracy—and bureaucratic elements are important in the electoral success of the Italian Social Movement today.

THE PARTIES IN 1968

The Christian Democrats emerged as the dominant party following the fall of Fascism. It is a much more broadly based party than the Popular party had been, and it includes many groups that took refuge in it as the party of order and stability. It is a religious party, but it is much more than that. It is the least class-based party in Italy, with a substantial lower-class following, especially in rural areas, as well as support from the middle and upper strata of society. It is especially the party of the old and of women. This reflects its religious base. Its lower-class

29

support, for example, is concentrated in those sectors that practice their religion. These include much of the peasantry, owner-farmer groups throughout most of Italy, and pockets of practicing working-class Catholics mostly in the northeast. As such, the DC is a confusing party in terms of ideology and interest. In philosophical terms it is of course Catholic, but there are several strands of political ideology within Italian Catholicism, and most of them are represented within the Christian Democratic party. The same problem applies to interests. The DC is heterogeneous in its socioeconomic following and hence in the interests to which it must appeal. Unlike the parties of the left, it cannot concentrate on the have-nots of society, and unlike its Liberal rival for middle-class votes, it cannot merely articulate the interests of the business community. Furthermore, it is the spokesman for the major agricultural organization in Italy, the Direct Cultivators, and is at least officially sensitive to agricultural interests. It is in fact torn by competing interests. Since it is the chief factor in public policymaking it is the target in the policy game of many groups that do not get much involved in the electoral game. As the dominant party of the country it follows a strategy that facilitates maintenance of this dominance.[29] It must maintain the proper mix of ideology, interest, and broad socioeconomic support. It is held together as much by the glue of power as any other adhesive.

The Liberal party has a much simpler task, but it pays a price in declining electoral fortunes and decreasing influence. It is the party of the upper-middle class, a designation it shares with the DC and other parties, but unlike the DC, its following is largely limited to this social class. It was in the past a secular party with a "radical" wing and was indeed radical in its concern for a secular state and political liberty. While it has made its peace with the Church politically, it still represents a secular conservative tradition in Italy. But its socioeconomic base and representation of the interests of the business community have made it difficult for it to play more than a defensive role in postwar politics.

The Monarchist tradition had weak organizational roots. Monarchist sentiments were exploited by local notables who manipulated the party in their interest. It was the most clientelistic of Italian parties. It later merged with the MSI in the *Destra Nazionale* (National Right).

The MSI likewise represents only a partial tradition, and it is one that was discredited by the historical record. Despite that, it has maintained a following that is a strange alliance of aging Fascist party members and officials, bureaucrats who had prospered under Fascism, southern notables, and young rowdies in search of violence and adventure. It resists easy classification by socioeconomic categories, interests, and subculture. Superficially, it has an ideology, derived from the Fascist experience, of nationalism, order, and the priority of the state over the individual. But it is difficult to specify what it really stands for. The simultaneous attempt to benefit from nostalgia for the Mussolini era and yet to avoid its negative image creates problems for the party.

The Republicans do not fit easily into the traditional left. Historical radicals, they are currently modernizing technocrats who are secular, bourgeois, and well educated. For many people they represent the conscience of governments and hence play a parliamentary role not proportionate to their meager electoral strength.

The Italian socialist tradition has chronically suffered from disunity and frequently from disarray as well. It has always contained a wide spread of opinion ranging from reformist to revolutionary. The socialists have been split into at least two parties during most of the republican period, and the issue of their relations with the Communists has been a major source of dissension. In 1968, the PSIUP (Italian Socialist Party of Proletarian Unity) was a small socialist party close to the PCI, while the PSI-PSDI consisted of the merged Socialists and Social Democrats. The merger involved little more than a confederation; local units remained separate and the planned complete union could never be achieved. The PSI-PSDI split again in 1969, largely along the lines of the component parties.

These parties are usually both more and less than is suggested by their labels. The PCI, for example, is the largest Communist party in the world after the Chinese and Russian. Yet, if the Chinese and Russian parties represent the Communist ideal type, then the PCI certainly is best understood as part of the Italian socialist tradition. If we accept the attitudes and expectations of most of its leaders, militants, and voters as expressed in interviews, it would seem to be quite different from these two ruling parties. The Italian socialist tradition is the first in voting strength and in organizational effectiveness in the country. The strongest organizational base within that tradition is occupied by the PCI, which is also the largest in electoral strength. It is important in understanding Italian communism that it be viewed as part of the socialist tradition rather than as merely the cynical agent of a foreign power.

In terms of socioeconomic base, the PCI is very much a lower-class party with most of its votes coming from the urban proletariat and the rural peasantry. The PSI, on the other hand, is somewhat less lower class. It has the support of much of the new middle class of salaried white-collar workers who have family ties with the lower socioeconomic categories. Both Communists and Socialists have substantial middle-class intellectual support that is not of great numerical significance but is important within the leadership; this is especially true within the Socialist party, whose leadership is largely middle class. In terms of ideology, Socialists and Communists share a common origin in Marxism, though the Socialists are sometimes labeled as revisionist. In our opinion, the term revisionist has little discriminating power today, as the PCI is also quite "revisionist"; hence we would prefer to say that there are differing interpretations of Marxism within these parties. The more fundamental disputes concern the role of the Soviet Communist party, democratic centralism, and parliamentary democracy, but these differences are today of diminishing programmatic, as opposed to historical, relevance.

The traditions discussed above all participated in the last elections before the rise of Fascism. They were also present at its downfall. And they were represented in parliament at the time of the field research in 1968.

3

The Italian Electoral System

At the time of the 1968 study, there were only two kinds of elections in Italy—national and local. National elections are called "political" elections (*elezioni politiche*) and local ones "administrative" elections (*elezioni amministrative*). In the former, citizens vote for lists and express preferences among candidates for the Chamber of Deputies and for a single candidate for the Senate. The latter are for representatives to the communal and provincial councils. Citizens of the five special regions (Sicily, Sardinia, Valle d'Aosta, Trentino–Alto Adige, and Friuli–Venezia Giulia) have long been voting for representatives to regional assemblies as well, and the other regions elected regional representatives for the first time in 1970. Although referenda were provided for in the 1948 constitution, none was actually conducted until the referendum on the repeal of the divorce law, held in May 1974. Over 59 percent of those who voted favored retaining the right to divorce. A referendum that abolished the monarchy was carried out in 1946.

The 1948 constitution gave the Chamber a five-year term and the Senate a six-year term, while permitting the dissolution of either house under certain conditions. But the Senate was always dissolved with the Chamber so that both have been replaced in the same elections. A constitutional amendment has regularized this practice by establishing a maximum five-year term for both houses. Before 1972, all parliaments had lasted the full five-year term, but the parliament elected in 1968 was dissolved more than a year in advance. The actual date of elections is set only at the time of dissolution and can fluctuate considerably.

Elections are administered by the Ministry of the Interior. Voting is from 6:00 a.m. to 10:00 p.m. on Sunday and from 7:00 a.m. to 2:00 p.m. on Monday. These are legal holidays and reduced fares facilitate travel. Voting booths are widespread, and access is seldom a problem. There are no provisions for absentee voting, a factor that causes considerable disruption to those Swiss, German, and other foreign industries that employ large numbers of Italian workers. Special polling booths are set up in hospitals and rest homes, and servicemen and sailors may vote in communes other than those of their legal residence.

Women voted for the first time in national elections in 1946. Voting age differs for the two houses; in 1968 it was twenty-one for the Chamber and twenty-five for the Senate. Effective in 1975, the voting age was lowered to eighteen for all elections except for the Senate, which retained the age twenty-five requirement. Voting is defined as a "civic duty," and nonvoters with inadequate explanations have the fact entered in their official records. The real reason for the high turnout, however, is that voting has become a deeply ingrained norm of Italian culture, and not the existence of the largely meaningless penalty. Turnout in the postwar period has ranged from a low of 89.1 percent in 1946 to 93.8 percent in 1953 and 1958.[1] True rates of participation are actually higher than this, because these figures are based on the total electoral rolls. In order to vote, electors must have certificates that are delivered to them by municipal authorities. Certificates not delivered are retained by the authorities until the polls close. The percentage not delivered because the elector could not be found is revealing concerning the turnout rate: in 1946, certificates not delivered were 5.4 percent of the total; in 1948, 3.5 percent; in 1953, 2.7 percent; in 1958, 2.7 percent; and in 1963, 3.0 percent. Regional differences are significant: The rate in Abruzzo in 1963 was 8 percent; in Molise in the same year it reached 14.9 percent. These are regions of heavy emigration, suggesting that many voters simply are no longer resident there and that the lists are inadequately updated. Out-of-date lists have been less of a problem in recent years as it has become easier to change one's official place of residence. The rate of participation goes up if it is recomputed on the basis of certificates delivered; for example, the Abruzzo increases from 86.5 to 94.8 percent and Molise from 79.5 to 94.4 percent.[2]

The ballot for a parliamentary election contains the symbol, or symbol and name, of each party presenting a list in the constituency. The party's position on the ballot in each constituency is determined by the date of filing its list in that constituency. Parties that have difficulty in agreeing on a list are thus penalized by being lower on the ballot, though the importance of position has not been adequately studied. The ranking of names on the list is determined by the party. There are no legal controls over a party's nominating procedure. Often, one or two well-known national leaders will head the list with others following in alphabetical order, but this is at the discretion of the party. Although the lists are widely publicized on official posters, the ballot itself contains no names of candidates, and preferences must be written in. One technique that may be important in areas of high illiteracy is to provide voters with a tiny stencil containing the name. In addition, the candidate's number on the list may be used instead of his name.

Election to the Chamber is by party list in constituencies that in 1968 ranged from four to forty-seven seats. These constituencies generally group together all the provinces of a small region or a part of a large region. They follow closely the administrative divisions of the country. However, the constituencies themselves seldom reflect fully the structure of normal party organization, which is largely by province, so that drawing up the list and managing the campaign in the constituency often present problems.

The election of senators is also in fact largely by proportional representation, in the following manner: Each region of Italy is allotted a number of senators proportional to its population with a minimum of seven, except for the sparsely populated regions of Molise and Valle d'Aosta, which are guaranteed minima of two and one senators. Each region is then divided into a number of districts of roughly similar size equal to the number of senators to be elected. Each party runs one candidate in each district. Anyone with 65 percent of the vote in that district is declared elected. Otherwise, the votes for all candidates of a party or group of parties in the region are pooled, and seats are assigned by proportional representation to the parties and then to the candidates who received the highest percentage of votes within their individual districts. This system permits parties to draw up joint regional lists. Thus the Social Proletarians and the Communists might agree that in district X the latter would put up no candidate while the former would run none in other districts. In this manner the Social Proletarians could obtain representation in the Senate and the Communists would be assured of additional votes in the region. This practice is of marginal importance. Most senators are elected by proportional representation with the region as the constituency; for example, in 1968 only two were elected by receiving 65 percent of the constituency vote—one from the Christian Democratic party and one from the Südtiroler Volkspartei.

As the Chamber and the Senate have similar powers and are elected at the same time, it is not surprising that they virtually duplicate one another. Yet, despite their constitutional equality, the Chamber is of greater political importance than the Senate. Most party leaders sit there and most ministers are chosen from the Chamber. The Chamber also receives more attention in elections.

The 1948 constitution provided for one deputy for every 80,000 electors. The number of seats in the Chamber consequently fluctuated upward, from 574 in 1948 to 596 in 1958. The number was permanently fixed at 630 for the Chamber and 315 for the Senate by constitutional amendment in 1963. The number to be elected in each constituency is adjusted for every election according to the latest population figures, and it is thus not necessary to redraw the constituency boundaries.

The major parties present lists throughout the country. This is not the same thing as mounting effective campaigns, and the smaller parties, especially the Monarchists and Republicans, often are barely visible outside of their areas of concentrated strength.

The nomination of candidates is a party matter, unregulated by law and unstudied by scholars. Technical problems of securing signatures make it difficult for casual lists to get on the ballot but the presence of sixteen parties on the Roman ballot in 1968, including the Pensioners' party, dissident leftists, local lists, and so on, suggests that the difficulties are not overwhelming.

The counting of votes involves the distribution of preference votes.[3] The elector votes for the party and may, if he wishes, list particular preferences. In constituencies electing fewer than sixteen he may mark up to three; in others, four. The number of candidates elected on a list depends on the total vote for that list, while the particular candidates elected are determined by the number of preference votes received. There are great differences in the extent to which the right to express a preference is exercised; for example, the rate varied in 1958 from 13.97 percent in the constituency of Milan to 51.04 percent in that of Palermo.[4] But this masks considerable differences among the parties, and it also means different things in different areas and parties. In much of the south, for example, the local organizations of the right and center parties, including the Christian Democratic, make arrangements with candidates to deliver them a certain number of preference votes. In this case the large number of preference votes cast reflects not only the greater personalization of politics but also the clientelistic nature of party organization.

In distributing votes among the party lists, a quotient is established for the constituency by dividing total vote by seats to be filled plus two, and seats are assigned to parties that meet multiples of the quotient. If this process would result in more deputies being seated than have been allotted the constituency, the quotient is computed again on the number of seats plus one, then plus none, until seats are assigned. Votes that do not contribute to the election of a candidate are transferred to the national electoral office, if the party received 300,000 votes nationally and elected at least one candidate in a constituency. Likewise, seats not distributed with the quotient of the number of seats plus none are transferred to the national electoral office. A national quotient is then established, and parties are assigned the remaining seats. However, there is no national list. Instead, parties rank unsuccessful candidates according to their number of preference votes. Thus a candidate who receives a large number of preference votes but is not elected on the constituency list still has a chance of being elected in the national college. Candidates who were elected in two constituencies, or to both the Senate and the Chamber, must opt for one or the other (they can run in up to three Chamber constituencies); the candidate with the next highest number of preference votes on the vacated list is then declared elected. Subsequent vacancies are filled in a similar fashion, avoiding by-elections. In the Valle d'Aosta, if no one receives a majority in the competition for the single Chamber seat, a runoff election is held two weeks later between the two leading candidates. For the Valle d'Aosta Senate seat a plurality suffices.

The Italian electoral system thus achieves proportionality to as great an extent as any system except those, such as the Netherlands and Israel, that essentially use the entire country as a constituency. Indeed, Rae has written that the only "law" of electoral systems is the "persistent bias of electoral laws in favor of strong parties as against their weaker competitors," but also that "the largest remainder formulae reduce the advantage of large elective parties over small ones to its lowest limit."[5] Moreover, the magnitude of the constituency is very important in determining the extent of fractionalization, which "increases at a decreasing rate as magnitude increases."[6] Most Italian constituencies are sufficiently large for fractionalization to be maximized; having larger constituencies would increase it only slightly. Moreover, the Italian method for distributing seats—which Rae calls the *imperiali* formula—contributes further to fractionalization. Thus the impact of the Italian electoral system is to encourage the proliferation of parties. However, it achieves a high degree of proportionality, which undoubtedly aids its legitimacy, and there are no serious proposals for altering it supported by substantial segments of the body politic.

The multimember constituency, preference votes, and party control over the composition of the lists place the party in almost complete control over who is and who is not elected. While the role of the party apparatus is crucial in all of the parties, it varies according to the strength of the central bureaucracy.

In the PCI, for example, the party organization nominates what is in effect a "balanced ticket" assuring representation to relevant territorial and socioeconomic categories. Party militants are then instructed as to whom to give their preference votes, and in general voters are encouraged to vote for the party rather than individuals. Although the PCI organization can greatly influence preference votes, it cannot, of course, control the total number of votes received. Thus it is only the marginal candidate, the *n*th one in the party's scale of importance, who cannot be certain of election. For the rest, election is no surprise once they have been nominated. The national leaders receive many preference votes; other candidates have only a small spread between them.

The same system works, though less effectively, within the socialist parties. The better-known party and factional leaders are usually assured the preference votes of the militants, whereas candidates without close organizational ties have little chance of election. The Christian Democratic party works somewhat the same way throughout most of Italy, though there are party notables who possess such a strong local or clientelistic base or support in non–party-affiliated organizations that they are not effectively controlled by the party. The Liberals and Monarchists are much more parties of notables, and the role of the organization is limited or nil. Little has been written of a scholarly nature about the organization and selection of candidates in the MSI. We will look more closely later at the nomination process in the three major parties.

In a system such as the Italian there is little competition between individual candidates of different parties. It is the party that counts, and the parties that are closest together in subcultural networks and policy preferences are the ones that compete most in elections. Within parties, there is a subtle competition for preference votes. Turnover of personnel between one parliament and the other thus represents different things in different parties. For the Communists it generally represents a deliberate attempt to keep the delegation young and representative of the diverse groups within the party. In the socialist parties it more likely represents shifting prestige of leaders within local and national party organs. In the DC it represents a combination of these factors. What it usually does not represent—in comparison with, for example, the United States—is the rejection by the public of particular individuals. It is true that important public figures are sometimes not reelected, but the reasons are likely to be found in intraparty politics; the most important party figures can be assured of election by being placed on the ballot in constituencies in which the party is very strong and being guaranteed the preference votes of the party militants.

These special Italian features are shared with many systems of proportional representation. They have influenced the design of this study in several ways, and especially in those in which it differs from designs applied in the Anglo-American countries. Thus the method of nomination, the competition both for party votes and for preference votes within the parties, and the dominance of the party organization emerge as important foci of the research.

TABLE 1
Votes and Seats in Chamber of Deputies Won in Italian Elections 1946–1976

	1946	1948	1953	1958	1963	1968	1972	1976
	Votes (%)							
Communists (PCI)	18.9 ⎫		22.6	22.7	25.3	26.9	27.2	34.4
Social Proletarians (PSIUP)	— ⎬ 31.0		—	—	—	4.4	1.9	—
Socialists (PSI)	20.7 ⎭		12.7	14.2	13.8 ⎫ 14.5		9.6	9.6
Social Democrats (PSDI)	—	7.1	4.5	4.6	6.1 ⎭		5.1	3.4
Republicans (PRI)	4.8	2.5	1.6	1.4	1.4	2.0	2.9	3.1
Christian Democrats (DC)	35.2	48.5	40.1	42.4	38.2	39.1	38.8	38.7
Liberals (PLI)	6.8	3.8	3.0	3.5	7.0	5.8	3.9	1.3
Qualunquists	5.3	—	—	—	—	—	—	—
Monarchists	2.8	2.8	6.8	4.8	1.7	1.3 ⎫	8.7	6.1
Neofascists (MSI)	—	2.0	5.8	4.8	5.1	4.4 ⎭		
Others	5.8	2.3	2.9	1.7	1.4	1.4	1.9	3.4
	Seats (House)							
Communists (PCI)	104	131	143	140	166	177	179	227
Social Proletarians (PSIUP)	—	—	—	—	—	23	—	—
Socialists (PSI)	115	52	75	84	87 ⎫ 91		61	57
Social Democrats (PSDI)	—	33	19	22	32 ⎭		29	15
Republicans (PRI)	25	9	5	6	6	9	14	14
Christian Democrats (DC)	207	305	263	273	260	266	267	263
Liberals (PLI)	41	19	13	17	40	31	21	5
Qualunquists	30	—	—	—	—	—	—	—
Monarchists	16	14	40	25	8	6 ⎫	56	35
Neofascists (MSI)	—	6	29	24	27	24 ⎭		
Others	18	5	3	5	4	3	3	14
% Voting of Those Eligible	89.1	92.2	93.9	93.7	92.9	92.8	93.1	*

SOURCE: 1946–1972—Thomas T. Mackie and Richard Rose, *The International Almanac of Electoral History* (New York: Free Press, 1974), pp. 219, 221; 1976—*Corriere della sera*. 23 giugno 1976.

*1976 turnout not available

4

Traditions, Networks, and Social Structure

Students of the comparative study of political behavior have learned a great deal about national variations in the importance of particular dimensions of political cleavage.[1] Thus it has been widely demonstrated that cleavage is rooted in the social structure of a polity and that country differences in the relationship between partisanship and social structure are likely to be found in the relative saliency of particular dimensions of cleavage. Differences such as social class and occupation reflect differing rates and patterns of industrialization and economic change. Cleavages over religion and language often have obscure historical origins that seem remote from the contemporary world. Differences in beliefs and values have a variety of origins. It is the manner in which these sources combine that defines the structural bases of political cleavage in particular countries. And it is the large number of possible combinations that makes national histories so varied and the task of the comparativist so complex. Italy has a highly idiosyncratic pattern of the structural bases of conflict, yet this pattern contains no single feature not shared with other polities.

The following analysis demonstrates that involvement in the social networks of religion and of the left are the most important variables in explaining partisan identification in Italy. Specifically, among the variables on which we have measures, religious observance and connections with a left trade union define the two poles of partisanship at the mass level. The two social networks associated with these poles serve to anchor mass partisanship, to institutionalize it, to give it the remarkable stability of the republican era. Other variables relating to social structure are not nearly as important as these two.

SOCIAL NETWORKS

It is a fundamental theme of Italian politics that the social networks of the left and of the Church dominate mass publics. Many consequences of this are widely understood; however, analysis of survey results uncovers some nonobvious and nontrivial consequences of this for representation.

The technique of "tree" analysis helps us to explore the role of these networks. Tree analyses are increasingly familiar in social science, and no extensive description is necessary here.[2] The object of tree analysis is to explain as much of the variance in the dependent variable as possible through repeated bifurcation of the branches into categories based on the independent variables. The present analysis is limited to socioeconomic variables. A large number were used, including occupation, union membership, strike behavior, social class, education, type of school attended, sex, marital status, age, length of residence, size of city, father's occupation, living standard of parents, father's political preference, income, region, organization memberships, and church attendance. The dependent variable—the one that is being "explained"—is identification with left parties (PCI, PSIUP, PSI-PSDI) as declared by the respondent.[3]

Figure 1 details the findings of the tree analysis. It was performed only with the 1983 respondents who expressed a party preference, 38 percent of whom chose parties of the left. The first bifurcation resulted in almost equal groups of those who claimed to attend church weekly and those who did not. Of the former, 17 percent voted for the left; of the latter, 58 percent. The portion of the total variance explained by this dichotomized variable is 18.1 percent. This confirms the primary role of religion in the political divisions of Italy. And if weekly church attendance is interpreted as meaning above all else insertion in the Catholic communications network, then the importance of organization is dramatically illustrated.

Another organization variable appears as the next branch in the tree—the presence of family ties with the *Confederazione generale italiana del lavoro,* or CGIL (the Communist-Socialist–oriented trade union), as measured by membership of the respondent or claimed for the head of the family by the respondent. This variable emerged empirically as the next most important one in both branches of the tree.

FIGURE 1
Tree Analysis of Left Partisan Identification

Total variance reduced by 28.3%.

Number in italics=Dependent variable:
    % identifying with PCI, PSIUP,
    and PSI-PSDI in 1968.

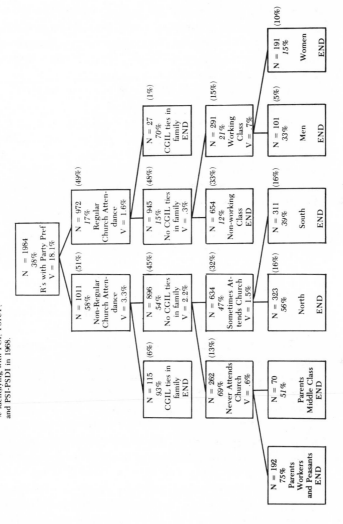

Among those who claimed regular church attendance, only twenty-seven respondents mentioned CGIL members in the family, and 70 percent of this cross-pressured group identified with parties of the left. Among nonregular churchgoers, the left identifiers rose to 93 percent of those with CGIL ties in the family. Within the latter group, frequency of church attendance again assumes importance, this time separating those who sometimes attend church from those who never attend. The former in turn divide between those with middle-class parents and those whose parents were workers or peasants. Among those who sometimes attend church the final split is between those resident in the north and in the south.

Among regular churchgoers without CGIL ties, the next split is between the working class, on the one side, and middle-class and agricultural respondents, on the other. Only the former group divides further, this time between men and women. Figure 1 shows the number in each category, the percentage of that category that identifies with the left, and the variance reduced by the variable, as a percentage of total. The total variance reduced by these seven variables, or six if the two different splits on the variable of church attendance are treated as a single one, is 28.3 percent.

In table 2 the nine categories into which the tree analysis has divided the sample are listed in order of the declining portion of that category that identifies with the left. Several other characteristics of the categories are also listed in this table. With the aid of the tree analysis and the groups that it has defined empirically it is possible to place the importance of several prominent socioeconomic variables in perspective.

Social network ties are more important than the commonly emphasized variables of social status, region, and sex. The largest single bloc consists of active middle-class and peasant Catholics, who are one-third of those identifying with a party. It is politically important that this group does not decompose into subgroups with much explanatory power. It is a religious bloc that seemingly rejects strongly the appeal of the left, and it is larger still when active Catholic working-class women are included. Active Catholic women are strongly nonleftist in their preferences regardless of social class; more than twice the portion of active Catholic working-class men than women support the left. Thus sex turns out to be an important variable for the 10 percent of the population classified as active Catholic working-class female. When this group is added to the 32 percent of the active Catholic nonworking-class population, there is a formidable religious bloc, comprising 42 percent of the identifiers, that gives its vote overwhelmingly to parties of the center and right.

The left has a similar substantial bloc in the CGIL union-affiliated respondents, but it is not comparable in size to the active Catholic bloc. Even if all of the unidentified Communist voters belonged to this category—which is an unwarranted assumption—the left would still be much smaller than the center and right.

Neither bloc, however, constitutes a majority of the population. Consequently, the one-third of the population that is not caught up closely in either of the networks holds the balance in the system. It is within this bloc that substantial differences emerge between north and south; in the north, 57 percent of those with loose church ties—that is, those who attend church, but irregularly—support leftist parties, while in the south only 41 percent do so. As 33 percent of the population falls into these two categories, these differences between north and south in support for the left are of prime political importance. And it must be emphasized that this emerges inductively from the tree analysis as one of the powerful explanatory variables.

Social class, which is widely viewed as a major explanatory variable in political behavior, likewise emerges as important in Italy, especially among people who are not all tied up in the structures of the two major social networks. The difference between the portion identifying with the left coming from middle-class (51 percent) and working-class (75 percent) backgrounds is substantial. This suggests that class assumes greater explanatory power when organizational and subcultural ties are minimized.

The preceding analysis identified several behavioral categories derived from a tree analysis of the vote for the left. It now must be shown how the party vote differs within these categories. All of the groups identified by the tree analysis divide their vote among virtually all the parties, but the wide spread in the portion going to particular parties identifies the central tendencies of the group in question. Table 3 gives the party division of the vote of each group, while table 4 gives the percentage that voters from each group form of the total vote of each party.

Several preliminary generalizations are in order. The first is that it seems to be much easier for the groups that attend church to support the PSI-PSDI than the PCI. Another is that, at least as measured in terms of declared party preference, the DC receives a higher percentage of support than the PCI in every group except the first three. Support for the PSI-PSDI, on the other hand, does not vary greatly

TABLE 2
Italy: Selected Indicators for Decomposed Electorate
(N = 2,500)

PERCENTAGE OF RESPONDENTS
(N in Parentheses)

GROUP LABEL	CODE GROUP TYPE LETTER	N	%	With Left Party Identification	Below Age 40	Without Party Identification	With Stable Voting Record	Very Close to Party	Very Close to Party among Those with Left Party ID	Very Close to Party among Those with DC Identification	Family Members in Unions	With Only Elementary Education	Working Class Identification
Nonregular church attendance CGIL ties in family	A	129	5	94 (110)	49 (63)	9 (12)	84 (108)	62 (80)	67 (74)	40 (2)	100 (129)	77 (99)	84 (106)
No church ties No CGIL ties in family Social origin worker or peasant	B	244	10	78 (149)	43 (104)	21 (52)	80 (195)	32 (78)	38 (56)	37 (14)	11 (27)	84 (205)	84 (199)
Regular church attendance CGIL ties in family	C	32	1	70 (19)	44 (14)	16 (5)	78 (25)	41 (13)	58 (11)	17 (1)	100 (32)	72 (23)	74 (23)
Loose church ties No CGIL ties in family North	D	432	17	57 (184)	39 (168)	25 (110)	82 (356)	24 (103)	28 (51)	29 (35)	18 (80)	74 (321)	68 (289)

		N	%	(41)	(47)	(16)	(6)	(19)	(31)	(22)	(64)	(37)	(39)
No CGIL ties in family Social origin middle class	E	408	16										
Loose church ties No CGIL ties South	F			66 (261)	75 (308)	14 (57)	36 (54)	38 (48)	31 (125)	24 (97)	73 (299)	44 (178)	41 (127)
Active Catholic Working-class male	G	119	5	82 (97)	81 (97)	10 (12)	30 (20)	26 (9)	26 (31)	15 (18)	88 (105)	34 (40)	34 (34)
Active Catholic Working-class female	H	238	10	87 (201)	92 (220)	12 (29)	48 (73)	17 (5)	37 (88)	20 (48)	87 (208)	40 (95)	15 (29)
Active Catholic Nonworking class	I	807	32	50 (389)	67 (545)	23 (189)	43 (219)	30 (29)	36 (288)	18 (153)	84 (676)	35 (286)	15 (95)

TABLE 3

Division of Group Vote by Party

(%)

		BEHAVIORAL GROUP								
PARTY	TOTAL SAMPLE	A	B	C	D	E	F	G	H	I
PCI	12	58	37	34	9	13	12	7	1	3
PSIUP	2	6	4	9	3	1	2	0	1	1
PSI-PSDI	16	20	18	16	29	25	16	22	10	7
PRI	1	1	2	0	1	4	1	0	0	1
DC	42	4	16	19	28	24	36	55	64	63
PLI	3	0	0	3	3	7	3	1	1	4
MON	1	1	1	0	0	0	2	0	1	0
MSI	2	1	1	3	2	2	4	0	2	2
NA	21	9	21	16	25	24	24	15	20	19
Total %	100	100	100	100	100	100	100	100	100	100
N	2,500	129	244	32	432	91	408	119	238	807

NOTE: Letters refer to groups identified in table 2.

from one group to another. Only in the active Catholic working-class female and nonworking-class groups does the PSI-PSDI following decline substantially. And the Socialists receive their peak support from groups that are not integrated into either of the networks. Because of their size and absence of strong organizational ties, these groups are pivotal. The PCI is more successful with this group in the south than in the north; the PSI-PSDI pattern is the reverse of the PCI. The DC is strong in the south.

TABLE 4

Division of Party Vote by Group

(%)

		PARTY								
GROUP	TOTAL SAMPLE	PCI	PSIUP	PSI-PSDI	PRI	DC	PLI	MON	MSI	NA
A	5	23	16	6	3	0	0	7	2	5
B	10	29	20	11	14	4	1	14	4	10
C	1	4	6	1	0	1	2	0	2	1
D	17	13	28	32	14	11	15	0	17	21
E	4	4	2	6	14	2	8	0	4	4
F	16	16	14	17	17	14	20	43	34	19
G	5	3	0	7	0	6	1	0	0	4
H	10	1	4	6	0	14	4	7	9	9
I	32	7	10	14	38	48	49	29	28	30
Total %	100	100	100	100	100	100	100	100	100	100
N	2,500	310	50	397	29	1,064	72	14	47	517

NOTE: Letters refer to groups identified in table 2.

When the group composition of the vote for individual parties is examined there are few surprises. The proportion of the party's identifiers coming from a particular group is of course limited by that group's proportion of the total sample, so that it is not the percentage alone that merits attention, but rather the absolute numbers involved. This latter information can be calculated from the first column in table 4, while the other columns relate the percentage of each party's identifiers contributed by the category.

Discovering the undeclared PCI identifiers from the breakdown by group is impossible. Apart from an expected tendency to concentrate somewhat in groups without strong organizational commitments, the respondents who would not or could not identify with a party are spread over all of the groups. Only the no-church-attendance–CGIL-ties group falls far below the all-group mean. This is understandable, for having acknowledged CGIL ties, little additional risk is incurred in acknowledging a preference for the PCI or other left parties. The dependence of the DC, PLI, and, to a lesser extent, the PRI, Monarchists, and MSI on peasant and middle-class church attenders is apparent, as is the importance of nonnetwork southerners to the Monarchists and MSI. The marginal differences in age among the various groups are important, as the left identifiers are younger and the practicing Catholics older (see table 2). In fact, the Catholic network is dominated by older citizens, and this contributed greatly to its decline in the years following 1968.

The existence of these social networks suggests several preliminary observations concerning the structural bases of partisanship. The first and most fundamental is that religion and social class, which are widely acknowledged to be important determinants of political choice in Italy, are not merely psychological objects or sociological categories for Italians. Religion and social class involve social networks of organizational ties and face-to-face contacts, as well as conceptual points of orientation for individuals. As a consequence, for respondents involved in one of these networks there are multiple sources of reinforcement in formal organizations, face-to-face contacts, socialization experiences, and ideological formulations. The determinants of partisanship are largely reinforcing. Few people are genuinely cross-pressured. No one need be involved at all levels. For the unsophisticated and less demanding, socialization and face-to-face contacts may provide all the anchoring that is needed. For others, additional supports are available. Politics is not a sometimes game played out at elections. For some it may hardly exist at all, yet their network cues enable them to vote "correctly," and to vote in very large numbers.

A majority of Italians fits into one of the major networks and its associated tradition. But the networks do not explain everything. Not everyone belongs, and those who do are integrated into them in varying degrees. The nature of the networks is changing under the impact of growing similarities in life styles and concerns. What history and ideology have torn apart, industrialization—that great simplifier—is putting back together again. But the separate organizations remain, the ideologies continue to diverge, children still grow up in one tradition or the other, or in none. However, Italian reality is too complex, and will remain too complex, to be grasped with simple formulations. The networks give us a point of departure; they provide no road map. Although they are an uncertain guide to understanding, they suggest new directions in the search for explanations of representation in Italy. The network underpinnings of the traditions and the parties that are their organizational expressions merit special emphasis.

PARTISANSHIP, RELIGIOUS PRACTICE, AND UNION MEMBERSHIP
The tree analysis has demonstrated the tremendous influence that religious practice and union membership have on partisanship in Italy. This influence can be documented even more dramatically by a direct examination of several components of religious behavior and union membership.

Italy is an overwhelmingly Catholic country. Religious minorities include about 50,000 Protestants, a small Jewish community, and only traces of other groups. In our mass sample, in 1968, 96 percent considered themselves to be Catholics. But among the two left elite groups, it is clear that religion is unimportant; indeed, as one moves left in politics and up in political hierarchy, atheism dominates the responses (see table 5).

As the tree analysis has demonstrated, church attendance is the best

TABLE 5
Does Respondent Consider Himself or Herself Catholic?
(%)

YES, R IS CATHOLIC	PARTY							
	PCI	PSIUP	PSI-PSDI	PRI	DC	PLI	MON	MSI
Mass	80	94	97	93	100	98	93	98
Councilors	27	—	77	—	99	—	—	—
Deputies	0	—	18	—	100	—	—	—

single predictor of partisanship. Table 6 shows the levels of church attendance of the identifiers and elites of different parties.

Several aspects of this close relationship between religion and politics merit closer scrutiny. We have previously noted that older respondents are more religious than younger. This obviously has consequences for religion and for politics. Before assuming that religion is likely to decline in importance with the passing of the older generation, another analytical problem must be confronted—the generation versus life-cycle explanation of cohort differences. The older respondents attend church more often. The percentage of the total sample that claims weekly attendance rises from 45 percent of those 21–29 to 60 percent of those 60–69. The older respondents also exhibit greater affect for the clergy, with the mean score for different age cohorts in our sample rising from 50 for those 21–29 to 60 for those 60–69.[4] The important question is whether older respondents were always more religious—a generational explanation—or whether people become more religious as they age—a life-cycle effect. With data from a single point in time we cannot answer this question. However, there are a number of reasons for assuming that a secular decline in religious attachment has been under way in Italy during the republican period. The most important are the increases in urbanization, education, and industrial employment, three trends that have been widely associated with a decline in religious attachments. As a result of these and other changes there has been a gradual change in the status of women, marriage, the family (and especially the extended family), and the role of religion in national cultural life. People attend church less regularly, and it seems to be more and more difficult for the clergy to influence electoral politics.

However, the Catholic subculture and the Christian Democratic electorate should not be equated. The latter is larger than the former. While there is no doubt that the Catholic subculture is the core of the DC, the party has many identifiers who share the tradition's emphasis on order and authority and support it politically for pragmatic rather than religious reasons. And many support it for immediate, policy-oriented reasons. In other words, there are multiple reasons for attraction to the DC; religious belief is only one, albeit the most reliable one. Because of the existence of these different levels of commitment, it is difficult to evaluate what might happen to the party if the trend toward a more secular society continues, if the depoliticization of the Church begun by Pope John XXIII bears fruit, and if religious practice continues to decline. These developments could spell disaster for the DC.

TABLE 6
Party Preference and Frequency of Church Attendance
(%)

PARTY

FREQUENCY	PCI		PSIUP		PSI-PSDI			PRI	DC			PLI	MON	MSI
	Mass	Councilor	Mass	Deputy	Mass	Councilor	Deputy	Mass	Mass	Councilor	Deputy	Mass	Mass	Mass
Weekly	12	3	20	0	28	11	4	38	69	78	96	54	36	38
Often	16	1	22	0	28	8	0	17	16	14	2	16	21	21
Sometimes	24	8	30	0	25	30	9	17	10	6	2	20	21	30
Rarely	24	10	16	0	12	18	4	10	4	1	0	9	7	6
Never	24	77	12	100	6	32	82	17	1	1	0	2	14	4
Total %	100	99	100	100	99	99	99	99	100	100	100	101	99	99
N	279	99	50	27	368	114	28	29	1,047	144	47	56	14	47

On the other hand, the freedom from the confines of strict orthodoxy that is implied by these developments might enable the party to deal more effectively with the needs of the society. It might evolve more in a "catch-all" direction, broaden the basis of its appeal without alienating its religiously motivated supporters, and compete effectively in a future polity in which the rigidities associated with the traditions at the time of our fieldwork have eroded. However, the decline of religious practice might also cause it to splinter between those segments wishing to defend a smaller (but still substantial—for it is unlikely that Catholicism in Italy will cease to be politically significant during the present century) Catholic subculture and others who prefer to play down its confessional basis and compete more aggressively on a programmatic and issue basis. In short, predictions are unwarranted because the future depends on how the DC, the Church, and other components of the system react to events.

The relationship between union membership and party preference is as clear-cut as that between religious practice and preference. The Italian labor movement is divided among a number of national confederations, each of which is tied, in varying degrees of closeness, to a political party. In the years following our 1968 survey the unions began to loosen their party ties and, in a very tentative fashion, to move toward cooperation among themselves. Despite these changes, unions remain in fact closely connected with their respective traditions even as their organizational links to parties become attenuated. At the time of our survey in 1968 these developments had not made much headway and the party-union relationship was relatively straightforward.

The Christian Democratic–oriented CISL (*Confederazione italiana sindacati lavoratori*) and the Communist-Socialist CGIL (*Confederazione generale italiana del lavoro*) were the two largest unions; the Republican–Social Democratic UIL (*Unione italiana del lavoro*) and Neofascist CISNAL (*Confederazione italiana sindacati nazionale lavoratori*) were much smaller. There were also several independent white-collar and agricultural unions independent of the four general confederations (though not without party ties). In its structure and functioning, Italian unionism resembles the French, rather than the American, variety. Several confederations are represented in the same factory or office; each puts up a list of candidates for plant council elections, and the returns are a good indication of relative union strength. Unions also have card-carrying memberships, but dues paying is irregular, and official membership figures are certainly inflated. It is ability to exert influence in strikes and through politics that counts, and throughout the years of the Republic before 1968 it was difficult to separate the trade union from the political-party aspects of much working-class action. The close ties between the union and the tradition channeled people into unions that were complementary to their parties. The strong tendency for members of particular unions to concentrate in particular parties is evident from table 7. The only mild surprise from the table is the involvement of the PSI-PSDI membership in all the union categories in roughly equal proportions. This reinforces other findings that the socialist mass is closer on many dimensions to the DC than to the PCI. Also important is the advantage that the DC obtains among the members of the "other" unions. These are mainly white-collar and agricultural unionists: of the 237 respondents in the "other" category, only twenty were in UIL and five in CISNAL. Since 91 percent of the CGIL group supported left parties, it is clear why membership in a left union is such a good predictor of partisanship.

TABLE 7

Party Preference and Union Ties of Respondent or Head of Household
Mass Sample
(%)

Party Preference	CGIL (Communist & Socialist)	CISL (Christian Democratic)	Other	None
PCI	59	5	5	13
PSIUP	8	0	2	2
PSI-PSDI	23	20	19	19
PRI	1	2	3	1
DC	7	70	61	58
PLI	0	1	7	3
MON	1	0	1	1
MSI	1	2	3	2
Total %	100	100	101	99
N	133	101	237	1,421

Religion obviously has a significant impact on union affiliation. For example, 56 percent of those who are members of, or have others in the family who are members of, the Catholic CISL claim to attend church regularly, while for the Communist-Socialist CGIL the figure is 20 percent. But Church and union are not the only structures of institutionalized tradition. In the postwar period a vast network of organizations existed to serve the Catholic tradition. Many of these were church related, such as the many Catholic Action groups; others were more narrowly political, such as the Direct Cultivators. This latter group organized independent farmers and served to channel governmental agricultural aid to the benefit of the DC. As a result of its patronage potential, it attracted or coerced the membership of many who did not share deeply the religious components of the tradition. Yet all of these organizations served to encapsulate the religious population in the Catholic political tradition. And of course the Church itself was for many the most salient component of the tradition. Bishops and priests did not hesitate to use the pulpit and the confessional for political counseling, and many people who were apolitical were guided into political activity by their advice and influence.

SOCIAL NETWORKS AND SOCIAL CLASS

The tree analysis reveals several important aspects of social class in Italian politics. It shows that class is a predictor of partisan identification, but weak compared with the networks; not surprisingly, it is more important for people outside of the two major social networks. These network ties affect the fit between class and partisan choice. Thus while it is obvious that left parties rely heavily on the working class, they also receive strong support from the middle class. And the Christian Democratic party draws massive support from the working class and peasantry.

No party is able to monopolize the votes of a class; while the PCI says that it is the party of the working class, the PSIUP, PSI-PSDI, and DC can all make this claim as well. In addition, the PRI and MSI attempt an interclass appeal. Moreover, the middle class spreads its votes, not only between the PLI and DC, but among the parties of the moderate left and the far right as well.

But class differences remain. Those members of the working class who support the PCI are unlike those who support the DC and the moderate left; there are important sex differences in the impact of social class; there are great geographical differences as well.

Social networks are useful in understanding the subtle interplay of social class with other aspects of social structure. In brief, the networks have held together for a long time what economic development threatens to pull apart. The contemporary significance of social class in Italy is greatly affected by the late industrialization of the country. In 1900, 58.8 percent of the economically active Italian population was engaged in agriculture; the tipping point into an industrial society was reached in 1931, when 50.6 percent of the active population was in the secondary and tertiary sectors of the economy. In 1952, about 42 percent were still in agriculture; in 1968, the year of our study, that figure had been cut in half—to about 20 percent. In that latter year, 57 percent of our sample said that their parents had agricultural occupations, and another 24 percent were children of workers. Hence a striking 81 percent of our sample were from worker or peasant families.

This delayed industrialization had several consequences for Italian politics. One was the immense population pressure on the land that drove 9,380,000 persons into emigration between 1876 and 1930 and caused 383,908 Italians to work abroad in 1960, mainly in Western Europe.[5] Another consequence of late industrialization was a failure of the new middle classes to carry out a revolution in mores and social structure. Small, insecure, and timid, the Italian middle class copied the social outlooks and life styles of the aristocracy; like previous Italian elites, it relied heavily upon traditional institutions such as the bureaucracy, army, and Church as instruments of social control. Like every other rule that Italy has experienced, the brief liberal rule resulted in no social revolution, did not greatly loosen the class structure, and ended with the liberals closely integrated into the traditional establishment, or establishments, for Italian elites were even more fragmented then than now. The modernization wrought by the liberals was a hothouse growth that needed constant tending by solicitous governments; it grafted a modern economic sector onto a social structure that was slow to change.

It was a traditional structure but not a feudal one. As a system of mutual rights and obligations, feudalism was not very significant in Italy. Traditional society took different forms in different parts of the country. A *contadino* is a peasant, but there was a vast difference between the peasant in the south with few rights and no security, who worked or rented land from absentee landlords, and the Tuscan sharecropper with hereditary rights and considerable security; the large farm that hired wage labor was common in the north; so was the small, poor, and proud independent landowning peasant of Piedmont and the northeast. Each of these economic systems gave rise to characteristic forms of organization and political action. The sharecropping system of central Italy led to collective action under leftist organizational leadership. In some areas of the north the Church took the lead in organizing the peasantry. In the south life remained the war of all against all.

The prolongation of Church influence into the present is closely related to the timing of economic development. The nature of traditional society varied; it is traditionalism itself, that is, resistance to change, that is the common thread in the complex social structure of Italy at the dawn of modernization. In areas with anticlerical traditions, such as Emilia and Tuscany, much of the peasantry was leftist; in many others the traditional society was greatly influenced by priests. The middle class exhibited the same internal divisions. The new *borghesia* was anticlerical and secular, but less so than its rhetoric suggests. Wives and daughters often attended church; indeed, in many areas and social strata, "goodness" among women is associated with religiosity, especially among the never married and the widowed. Even in many areas of high religious observance it was uncommon for adult males to frequent the Church. These sex and area differences in observance remain today.

Italian cities have sustained a vital urban life since classical times, despite variations in opulence and population; artisans, servants, and a *sottoproletariato* form categories that fit neatly into neither the agricultural nor modern industrial systems of social stratification. Artisans in particular have played an important role in the history of the Italian left.

In the early years of industrialization the Church had no viable social program. In the older industrial centers the emerging proletariat was largely lost to organized religion. However, there has always been a population exchange between city and countryside, as well as some continuity in urban religious observance, and these have resulted in the presence of a substantial number of practicing Catholics, especially women, within the urban working class. In areas that have been industrialized more recently, as in the smaller communes of the northeast, the Church has been more successful in maintaining its influence within the working class. In all cases, what is important is that the network, once established, can continue to exert a strong hold on individuals within it regardless of changes in social structure. Thus the left can attract nonpolitical wives, and the Catholic network incorporates secular-minded businessmen as well as militant trade unionists. The traditions have shown great continuity through time, with the result that partisan choice reflects the weight of history as well as the logic of contemporary social structure.

The following analysis will examine the relationship between social class and partisan choice including, where possible, data on elites as well as the mass public. We will document the extent to which the political class deviates from the mass level adherents on measures of social class. Since we hold that what is in fact represented is the tradition, we do not assume any necessary desirability of a socioeconomic fit between elite and mass. Nevertheless, in the light of the divisions of Italian politics the similarities within the political class are impressive.

We are using several indicators of social class. Table 8 indicates the occupational class of the mass publics, communal councilors, and deputies, by party. It is clear that party elites do not reflect the occupational composition of their party's identifiers. There is nothing surprising about this, as it is characteristic of all liberal democracies. Furthermore, it is clear from the research of the group led by Sartori that this has been the Italian pattern throughout the period since the Second World War.[6] It is evident that party elites are more similar in socioeconomic status to one another than to their respective mass publics.

The similarity of the communal councilors is especially striking given the Communist working-class bias. PCI councilors are surprisingly middle class in occupational status.

Many deputies of all parties claim political occupations, which fit uneasily the usual categories, but they do embody prestige, status, income, and life-styles that are far closer to the middle class than to the working class. Hence even though many of these Communist deputies were originally workers, they nevertheless are hardly simple proletarians by the time they enter parliament. The higher occupational status of the socialist and Christian Democratic deputies is apparent, as is the predominance of upper-middle-class occupations among the former and lower-middle-class occupations among the latter.

At the mass level the high status of the secular moderate parties is evident. Equally clear is the relatively low status of the Monarchists and Missini (MSI). Finally, party differences are important in the category of housewives, students, and unemployed, in which housewives predominate; the secular moderate parties do not recruit well in this weighty category.

We have already remarked on the impressive continuity of political traditions; here we will examine shifting patterns by age. As we must face the generation versus life-cycle problem, we cannot ascertain whether or not the young will retain these partisan orientations as they age. But it is clear that the left does bettter among the young than the old, though there are important class distinctions (see table 9). We simplified the occupational categories by dividing respondents into white collar, blue collar, and those without occupations and created age categories of 21–39, 40–59, and 60 and over. This analysis reveals considerable differences in the impact of age and occupation. Thus the Christian Democratic share of the vote remains constant in the white-collar groups but declines among the young in the blue-collar category and rises among the old in the "other" category. Most of the "other"

TABLE 8
Occupation of Respondent
(%)

	PCI			PSIUP	PSI-PSDI			PRI	DC			PLI	MON	MSI
	Mass	Coun-cilor	Deputy	Mass	Mass	Coun-cilor	Deputy	Mass	Mass	Coun-cilor	Deputy	Mass	Mass	Mass
Professional, managerial, industrialist, etc.	1	23	7	2	4	25	57	17	3	34	31	15	0	6
White-collar employee, small businessman, artisan, shopkeeper	13	57	19	14	22	68	11	34	18	63	43	24	7	19
Farm owner	5	4	0	12	3	0	0	0	4	1	0	3	7	0
Farm laborer	9	2	0	14	7	0	7	7	6	0	2	6	7	0
Skilled laborer	17	12	7	20	18	5	0	10	8	1	2	4	0	19
Unskilled laborer	15	2	0	12	9	2	0	0	4	1	0	4	0	4
Housewives, students, unemployed	40	0	0	26	37	0	0	31	57	0	2	44	79	48
Party and public officials	0	0	67	0	0	0	25	0	0	0	20	0	0	0
Total %	100	100	100	100	100	100	100	99	100	100	100	100	100	100
N	310	90	27	50	397	109	28	24	1,064	133	45	72	14	47

TABLE 9
Age and Party Preference in 1968, by Occupational Class
(%)

PARTY PREFERENCE	White Collar			Blue Collar			Other (Housewives, Students, Unemployed)		
	Under 40	40–59	60+	Under 40	40–59	60+	Under 40	40–59	60+
PCI	8	4	4	22	17	13	15	14	9
PSI-PSDI	19	17	11	18	21	15	9	13	7
DC	43	45	43	32	33	45	45	50	68
Other parties	31	33	42	27	29	27	31	22	16
N	413	342	153	350	391	269	222	205	140

category are housewives, especially among the older respondents, and they vote heavily Christian Democratic. The left in general does better among the young, with the Socialists benefiting most among white-collar youth and the Communists among blue collar. Curiously, the vote for "other" parties rises with age within the white-collar group, remains constant among blue-collar workers, and declines within the "other" occupational category. This is because older housewives are more strongly DC, while older white-collar voters more often support the parties of the right.[7]

The importance of class identification is shown by an analysis of subjective social class. This variable is based on the respondent's answer to the question, "To which social class would you say you belong?" If the response was not middle class or working class, the respondent was asked further, "Then would you say that you belong to the working class or to the middle class?" Rather than a generation or life-cycle problem, here we face the chicken-and-egg problem: does a respondent support the left because he thinks of himself as belonging to the working class? Or does he think of himself as belonging to the working class because he feels himself to be "leftist" in politics? Among individuals with white-collar occupations, subjective class identification seems to make little difference; within the blue-collar group, those identifying with the working class are more likely to support the left (see table 10).

The differences between the parties in subjective social class identification are important at both the mass and elite levels (see table 11). What is most surprising is the working-class identification of so many leftists with white-collar occupations, especially at the elite level.

The fit between social class and partisan preference is further complicated by education. Educational achievement expressed in terms of years of formal schooling has in the past been very closely related to social class. This is undoubtedly changing under the impact of the educational reforms of the 1960s, which raised the school-leaving age, modified the rigidity of the secondary-school programs, and opened up the universities to types of secondary-school diplomas heretofore denied admission. These reforms will undoubtedly have an impact on the relationship between education and social class. But in 1968 the impact of these changes lay in the future. At that time Italian education closely reflected the stratification system of the past.

Most Italians—75 percent of our mass sample—received only five years or less of formal education; that is, they went no further than elementary school. At the end of that stage the basic decision was taken concerning a university preparatory course. They could attend either a technical school that would complete their education or a middle school that could lead to the *liceo*; an alternative path led to business school instead of the *liceo* during the secondary school years or to schools that prepared them for elementary school teaching, artistic careers, or specialized technical careers. The *liceo* course itself was divided into classical and scientific paths, with the former emphasizing

TABLE 10

*Party Identification in 1968, by Occupational Class and
Subjective Social Class*

(%)

OCCUPATIONAL CLASS

PARTY	White Collar		Blue Collar	
	Subjectively Middle Class	Subjectively Working Class	Subjectively Middle Class	Subjectively Working Class
PCI	6	5	13	22
PSIUP	1	1	3	3
PSI-PSDI	16	17	15	21
PRI	3	1	1	1
DC	44	45	42	32
PLI	5	4	1	2
MON	1	1	*	*
MSI	3	2	2	1
Other	21	23	23	19
Total %	100	99	100	101

*Fewer than 5 cases.

TABLE 11
Occupational Class and Subjective Social Class, by Party
(% with Working-Class Identification)

OCCUPATIONAL CLASS	PCI			PSIUP	PSI-PSDI			PRI	DC			PLI	MON	MSI
	Mass	Coun-cilor	Deputy	Mass	Mass	Coun-cilor	Deputy	Mass	Mass	Coun-cilor	Deputy	Mass	Mass	Mass
White collar	72	52	39	60	45	28	9	12	38	11	19	4	*	22
Blue collar	95	95	100	84	86	87	50	75	84	80	33	78	*	79

*Denotes fewer than 5 cases.

Greek and Latin while the latter omitted Greek. Graduates of a classical *liceo* could enter any field; scientific *liceo* graduates were more restricted. Business school graduates could only enter the faculty of economics, and graduates of other specialized secondary school courses were similarly restricted at the university level or, in some cases, denied access to higher education.

The result of this system was a status ranking of courses of study, with the graduates of a classical *liceo* and a university at the top. Entry into almost all occupations was tied in closely with the educational system. For example, the governmental bureaucracy itself was, and still is, rigidly stratified, with educational attainments defining the level of entry and with virtually no transfer between strata. Entry into the Italian upper-middle class was difficult without the certification provided by a university degree. The importance of a university degree combined with the nature of secondary and university training to give rise to an intellectual and political elite sharing particular characteristics that are important for understanding Italian politics. At both the secondary and university levels, abstract thinking, historical and philosophical argument, and formal knowledge—often memorization of factual materials—are emphasized. Verbal facility is rewarded; examinations are largely oral and completely so at the university level. While scientific education is available, it is humanistic subjects that are emphasized. Except for history, social science is largely ignored. Subjects are not oriented toward training in problem solving or practical matters. The graduate of the system is well equipped to deal with abstract thinking and philosophical debate; furthermore, he is conversant with classical civilization and with his own national cultural heritage. It is a system that encourages a politics of verbal gymnastics, ideological debate, and—despite ideology—cultural elitism, for only the educated elite possess the skills in symbol manipulation that are a prerequisite for entry into the "political class." Even parties of the left that include nonuniversity graduates among their deputies usually do not assign them important roles. In a system in which political debate has traditionally taken the form of attacking and defending the values of the tradition—using the intellectual tools of high culture—even a party that is ideologically egalitarian feels the need for the legitimization that is provided by sophisticated cultural spokesmen.

Thus, like most European political systems, the Italian system is one in which most university graduates support the center and right, but in which each party is dominated by a well-educated leadership cadre that does not reflect the educational profile of the rank and file (see table 12). Party elites share an educational experience that undoubtedly leaves an impact on the political system. This education does not have the same effect on everyone, of course, and Communists, Socialists, Catholics, and Liberals emerge with quite different views. The impact is greatest on the *agenda* and *style* of politics. It contributes to the ideological nature of Italian political style, an aspect that certainly has changed somewhat over the past generation but that shows no signs of disappearing from the Italian scene. And it also contributes to a national tendency to favor the ideologue, the cultural spokesman, over the technocrat, the organizer, the pragmatic doer. These latter skills are of course necessary, and successful politicians must possess them in some measure in Italy as elsewhere. Furthermore, the growing importance of mass party organizations in the past generation has granted an increasing role to the organization functionary in all of the parties. But the importance of education remains, and especially significant is the difference in the levels of education possessed by elites and masses.

TABLE 12
Education and Party
(% with Some University Education)
PARTY

	PCI	PSIUP	PSI-PSDI	PRI	DC	PLI	MON	MSI	Total
Mass sample	*	2	5	14	4	27	0	15	5
Councilor sample	26	—	41	—	57	—	—	—	43
Deputy sample	38	—	84	—	78	—	—	—	71

*Less than 1 percent.

This chapter has demonstrated the central role played by the networks of religion and the left in mobilizing the population. Religious observance and family ties with a left trade union are the two most powerful variables in explaining partisan choice in Italy. Variables that have been demonstrated to be important in other countries, such as social class in particular, are less important than these two networks; these networks tie people into the political traditions of Italy.

5

Continuities in Partisanship

Against the background of extensive disruption, economic development, and population movement, the persistence through time of Italian political traditions is remarkable. The major forces that are present
on the Italian political scene today were largely present in the 1920s,
and their outlines were quite clear in the later years of the nineteenth
century. Lipset and Rokkan have argued that this is a general characteristic of European party systems: "The party systems of the 1960's
reflect, with few but significant exceptions, the cleavage structures of
the 1920's.... the party alternatives, and in remarkably many cases
the party organizations, are older than the majorities of the national
electorates."[1] That this should be the case in the stable democracies of
Western Europe is less surprising than its applicability to Italy. For
Italian electoral results have been stable during the republican period
despite extensive population replacement and geographical and social
mobility. In fact, taking account of changes in name, mergers, and
schisms, the partisan preferences of the electorate in 1968 were similar
to those of half a century previously. Continuity in traditions has been
stronger than for parties, as there has been substantial alteration of the
organizational structures that mobilize particular traditions.

In this chapter we will examine aspects of the continuity through
time of the partisanship of the Italian electorate. We begin with a
discussion of some conceptual problems encountered in dealing with
continuity and change.

GENERATIONS AND ITALIAN POLITICS

In the study of intergenerational continuity and change it is customary to differentiate among differences due to enduring change between one generation and another, differences due to cohorts being at different stages in the human life cycle, and differences reflecting the effect of a particular historical era. These are conventionally labeled generation, life-cycle, and period effects.[2] The term "generation effect" indicates that cohorts are different and will remain different as they age; a "life-cycle effect" means that as the younger cohorts age they become more like the old, so that cohorts are roughly similar as they pass through the same stages of their life cycles; a period effect reflects the impact of historical experiences that affect all the cohorts living at that time.

It is common in the study of politics to find that the values and behaviors of individuals are greatly affected by the atmosphere of the period in which they developed their awareness of politics. For example, Butler and Stokes have written, "We must ask not how old the elector is but when it was he was young."[3] And according to an Arab proverb, "Men resemble the times more than they do their fathers." At the same time, it is obvious that people—or at least electorates— change. Change takes place through the interaction of life-cycle, generation, and period effects, and this interaction often becomes quite complicated in polities that lack continuity in the political system. Yet political behavior in Italy possesses a remarkable continuity that is not easily explained by the conventional focus on political socialization and the parent-child transmission of partisan identification.

We believe that it is the institutionalization of the various political traditions that insures this continuity. Religious and other networks serve to perpetuate patterns of partisanship. These networks cut across class lines, so that class is less important than is often assumed; the left appeals to a segment of the middle class while the Christian Democratic party has quite substantial support within the working class, especially among women, peasants, and workers from less industrialized areas of the country. These networks reflect different historical periods. Like language or ethnicity in other countries, religious orientation in Italy is related to the preindustrial social structure and stratification system and has enormous influence today in those sectors of the society, such as peasants, women, and inhabitants of the geographical periphery, that have been relatively insulated from the secularizing influences of industrialization.

There are several societal institutional devices that seem to perpetuate the traditions regardless of economic change. Education is one. Education is not equally available throughout Italy today, and it was scarce in the past. Even in 1968 about three-fourths of the population had only five years or less of formal education. And Italian elementary education is strongly influenced by the Church and is positively correlated with Christian Democratic votes: The expansion of universal primary education has in fact served to reinforce the strength of the Church. On the other hand, the DC vote has been negatively correlated with the number of illiterates, secondary school graduates, and university graduates.[4] High technology requires high levels of educational achievement, while affluence makes possible and even desirable the prolongation of formal education. This has resulted in a substantial expansion of higher education, but without its yet having had much impact on politics. Although Italy today is about at the European average in the proportion attending the universities, the separate youth culture in 1968 was not as developed as, for example, in the United States. Many Italian university students attend part time, and almost all of them live at home. While students have been prominent in the extremist parties, they are also very active in the other parties as well.

The political role of Italian women has encouraged continuity. Women received little formal education during the youth of the older portions of our sample. When this is combined with the modal role expectations of the Italian wife and mother and limited contacts outside the circle of the immediate family, it greatly increases the likelihood that Italian women will support traditional rather than radical parties. Even if they do this for conventional reasons and not because of ideology or program, the consequences are to strengthen the nonleftist parties and especially the Christian Democratic party.

Social class as it is conventionally used today is essentially an industrial variable; despite the reality of class distinctions in traditional agricultural society, and notwithstanding the revolutionary potential exhibited by the peasantry in numerous countries, Italian revolutionary sentiments have made headway among the peasantry mainly in those areas in which a strong anticlerical tradition predated the growth of industry, as in the Red Belt of central Italy. Thus, at least for most of Italy, the political saliency of class is a product of the Industrial Revolution, and it has had its greatest electoral impact in areas that have been most affected by industrialization or those in which a radical tradition associated with industrialization has been grafted onto an anticlerical tradition. The generational cleavage that is potentially present in all societies cuts across the religious and class cleavages and has an impact different from others. Because of the strength of the subcultures and organizations—both of which cut across age cohorts—the generation gap in Italy seems to be smaller than it is in other advanced industrial societies. The Catholic subculture and organizations are intergenerational as well as interclass, and the left subculture and organizations are likewise intergenerational and, to a lesser extent, interclass.

It is doubly important that in advanced industrial countries the generation gap is especially large within groups most exposed to affluence and higher education. Since these groups are numerically small in Italy, and because the strength of the subcultures limits the independent impact of education, the generation gap in politics has been minimal. Although the young are often more radical than the old, in Italy they have generally worked within the dominant traditions. For example, while the parties of the left have repeatedly had difficulties with their youth and student movements, they have usually managed to retain control over them and eventually to incorporate most young dissidents into the adult movements. And a similar process has taken place in the Christian Democratic party, though its radicalism has been muted. The important point is that much youth revolt has taken place within the traditions, seeking to revitalize but not to repudiate them.

The cost of nonconforming politics can be great in Italy. The importance of personal contacts makes Italy less of a meritocracy than, for example, the United States, and the necessity for political connections in many sections of public and private employment provides the major parties with tremendous advantages. New political movements find it difficult to break into the existing distribution of political resources.[5] The result has been an amazing political continuity between cohorts despite massive social change and political discontinuities. The institutional structure of the society, the existing subcultures, and patterns of socialization channel people into the principal political traditions.

However, change can take place even within the existing structure. While learning takes place throughout the lifetime, early imprints are often very durable. For example, similar experience may make a different impression on the young and the old; for the mature, the new is grafted onto the old against the background of accumulated experience and is evaluated accordingly; for the young, it is likely to have a greater impact because of their less well-formed cognitive structure.[6]

Thus the young tend to be more open to the influence of new experiences even if everyone receives similar exposure to them. The formative years of different generations inevitably fall into different historical eras even if the formal socialization processes are constant. This insures that political culture is transmitted unevenly: Regardless of what is taught, what is learned is less than the whole of the existing political culture. Considerable alteration in content and subjective meaning takes place in the transmission. As cohorts pass from the scene and new ones enter, the content of the political culture alters, even without dramatic generational gaps.

The transmission of political culture is also affected by the differential rate of reproduction among social groups. Typically, the less modern segment has higher birthrates, though this is not inevitably the case. When religious values encouraging high fertility are superimposed on traditional and agricultural values, the differential in fertility between the rural and urban sectors may be very great, as in Quebec and other traditionalist Catholic areas. Italian differences in fertility can hardly be said to be specifically religious in origin since the country is overwhelmingly Catholic, at least in the formal sense. But they do affect the intergenerational transmission of cultural values, for the Italian regions that are least industrialized have the highest birthrates.

The demographic advantage accruing to traditional elements is minimized by the transformations of social structure that accompany industrialization and economic development. Traditional values, attitudes, and expectations are part of a traditional culture. While some may survive alterations of the traditional society, the total outlook is likely to change as the structures underpinning tradition erode under the impact of economic development. Changes in the family, in patterns of authority and social control, in the consequences of breaking old norms—all these combine to affect the nature of the transmission of the traditional culture. New social groups arise, such as technicians and scientists; previously existing ones, such as white-collar workers and the new salaried middle classes, acquire greatly increased numerical importance; traditional categories such as peasants, land owners, and the older middle class decline in size and importance.

Values and beliefs have a social location, and their political significance varies with the size and influence of the groups that espouse them. Moreover, to a remarkable extent their perpetuation seems to be dependent on the continued insertion of individuals within the particular social context. In an analysis of Italian survey data, Barnes and Sani have demonstrated that most attitudes and behaviors of southern-born Italians who have moved to the north are similar to those of northerners born in the north rather than to southerners.[7] Many political aspects of those patterns of thought and behavior associated with a traditional society are abandoned when the traditional society is left behind, suggesting that many cultural traits are heavily structurally dependent. Of course, the issue is much more complex than is implied here. There is considerable evidence that out-migration is highly selective, with dissidents and modernizers more likely to leave.[8] Nevertheless, it is likely that mobility has contributed greatly to changes in individual values and behaviors.

We have mentioned the importance of different life experiences of generations. The Fascist experience, World War II, changes in the mass media, general affluence, and extensive geographical mobility have affected generations differently. The young in most advanced industrial countries have been exposed to a far wider range of experiences than were their elders in their youth. The generally greater affluence has seemingly altered attitudes toward economic security and deprivation as well, at least for a substantial segment of youth and for the university educated in particular.[9] This is accentuated in Italy by the particular mix of continuity in the political system.

Most discussions of political socialization assume that there is an ongoing system into which individuals are socialized, yet the actual situation of most people in the world in this century is one of great discontinuity in the political systems under which they live. Discontinuity has been especially great in Italy. Older Italians living today knew three distinct governmental systems, which we will call regimes: the parliamentary monarchy, fascism, and the present republic. We have pointed out previously how each of these has left traces that are institutionalized in the parties and institutions of the present. Despite considerable institutional survival from one to another, the ethos of each regime was different.

The main point emphasized here is a simple one: In a country experiencing the degree of change that Italy has undergone, the political socialization experiences under one regime may not be a very good guide to political behavior under another. In periods of rapid and significant change—and change in a regime is certainly a very significant change—what is learned during youth may not be as important for behavior as what happens later in life.[10] Indeed, it could be argued that the learning that takes place closest in time to the behavior is likely to be more important; that is, adult learning should be more important than childhood socialization when the discontinuities in the institutional context of behavior are great. Against this background of change and discontinuity in regime, Italy's postwar partisan stability has been remarkable. We will examine several possible sources of this stability, the first of which is the family itself.

INTERGENERATIONAL TRANSMISSION OF PARTISANSHIP

The intergenerational transfer of partisanship has been well documented by political research. Numerous studies have demonstrated that American children acquire their political labels early in life.[11] And evidence is accumulating that these findings are true for other countries as well. Given the central role of the family in Italian life, it could be expected that the family would have a strong influence on partisanship.

However, the cross-cultural evidence is sometimes contradictory. Converse and Dupeux uncovered remarkable cross-national differences in children's knowledge of their father's partisan identification.[12] The possession of a partisan identification by French children who knew the political tendency of the father was similar to that in the United States: 79.4 percent in France and 81.6 percent in the United States. But the percentage of the population that knew the political tendency of the father in France was only one-third that of the United States (24 percent against 75 percent). And the percentage possessing a partisan identification among those who did not know their fathers' tendencies was roughly similar in the two countries: 47.7 percent for France and 50.7 percent for the United States.[13] The many changes in party name in both Italy and France complicate discussions of parent-child continuity in identification. Even so, it is clear that there are important national differences in the way in which the political socialization process functions and that consequently there are differences in the degree to which citizens are either locked into or not locked into the political system. Converse and Dupeux note that the absence of party loyalties in France leads to "current availability of a mass base for flash party movements under circumstances of distress," thus linking French political turbulence to the inadequate transmission of partisan loyalties from generation to generation.[14]

In a later article, Converse developed a model of partisan stability that relates the level of identification with a political party to four different processes: a *learning process*, reflecting experience with the party system; a *resistance* phenomenon, representing the difficulty of learning as one ages; a *transmission* process, from one generation to the next; and a *forgetting* process, during periods of nondemocratic rule.[15] As this model makes length of acquaintance with a party the most important variable, it accounts for variations arising from changes in regimes, absence of female suffrage within the older cohorts, and discontinuities in parties due to changes in name, mergers, splintering, and so on.

The model is useful for explaining differences in levels of partisan identification among various Italian cohorts, for our findings are compatible both with this model and with our view that representation in Italy is oriented around institutionalized traditions. Partisanship, the possession of a partisan identification, was higher in 1968 than at the time of *The Civic Culture* study in 1959; in fact, it was exactly double the earlier figure, increasing from 38 percent to 76 percent.[16] It is not immediately clear why this should be so. Perhaps the differences in wording alone can account for the unexpected results, for *The Civic Culture* questions, on which Converse's scoring of partisanship was based, asked, "Now we would like to find out something about your party preference and how you vote. Are you currently a member of any political party or organization? (IF NO) Toward which political party do you lean?"[17] Our questions in the 1968 study were, "To which party do you habitually feel closest?" and "Would you say that you feel very close to this party, more or less close, or not very close?" We also asked, "Are you a member of a political party? (IF YES) Which?" Intuitively, we do not think that the formulation of the questions alone is responsible for the differences. The high degree of institutionalization for the various Italian political traditions seems a more convincing explanation for the rapid increase in partisanship. Converse noted that "if politicized mass organizations tend to stimulate the development of partisan loyalties as is frequently supposed, then a society pervaded by such organizations to an unusual degree might be expected to display unusual speed in the mobilization of aggregate loyalties."[18]

The increase in partisanship reflected in the Almond-Verba data from 1959 and our 1968 data is undoubtedly due in part to the time elapsed that enabled the electorate to "learn" partisanship. Our data show that the percentage feeling "very close" to their party increases monotonically with age after age forty, rising from about 30 percent to almost 45 percent; between twenty-one and forty it fluctuates within a few points of 30 percent. But it is probable that nonparty attachments are at least as important as age itself in the development of stable partisanship. For example, older women form the least politicized of Italian cohorts, and they contribute heavily to the low ranking of Italy on measures of participation. At the same time they are, comparatively speaking, extremely religious. They are very close to the Church and because of that fact are quite consistent in their voting for the Christian Democratic party. But it is not the party that they feel close to; hence the stability of their attachment to the Catholic tradition is not captured by the way in which the Converse model is operationalized, for their attachment is not primarily political. From the point of view of political stability conceived in terms of attachment to party alone, this model is correct. If the Church were to withdraw its endorsement the Christian Democratic party would lose the current high level of support of those whose primary loyalty is to the Church and not the party. On the other hand, in terms of stability of the vote and of the political system under present conditions, the existence of loyalty to the tradition has the same effects as loyalty to the party. It is just that it is not necessarily or primarily political.

It is evident that the social networks of parties, Church, and unions must exert a tremendous influence on the direction of partisanship. Either the Italian's recall of his father's political preferences is very poor, compared with the American's, or forces other than paternal influence are pushing him in a particular partisan direction. For, unlike the French findings, there is little difference in the partisanship of those who do and those who do not recall the partisan leaning of their fathers (see table 13). What needs to be explained is the combination of low knowledge of father's identification with seemingly high stability in partisanship. The existence of low levels of knowledge is not difficult to understand. After all, Frenchmen exhibited similarly low levels even though they did not suffer as many or as lengthy discontinuities in the socialization process as the Italians. But the French electorate has been remarkably fickle, while the Italian has been constant in the division of the vote among the parties. It is always possible that it is only the marginal frequencies that have remained constant in the Italian vote, masking massive party switching. Undoubtedly switching does take place, and we are aware of the limitations of recall data concerning past voting. Nevertheless, 75 percent of our sample claimed to have al-

TABLE 13

Respondent Knows Father's Party Preference—Respondent Has a Party Preference

	Knows Father's Party Preference	Does Not Know Father's Party Preference
Percentage having a party preference	86	72
Percentage not having a party preference	14	28
Total %	100	100
N	673	1,827
Percentage of total electorate represented by N	27	73

ways voted for the same party in national elections.[19] There is considerable variation by party, with the major parties having the most loyal electorates (see table 14). As the Christian Democrats and the Communists have been the two poles of the system, it is not surprising that the electorates of other parties have switched more often.

TABLE 14
Percentage Always Voted Same Party in National Elections

Party	Percentage	N
PCI	79	221
PSIUP	62	31
PSI-PSDI	70	259
PRI	69	20
DC	83	872
PLI	52	29
MON	70	10
MSI	72	34
Mean	75	1,476

The two largest parties seem also to have gained the most in party switching between father and child. These figures must not be overinterpreted, for the numbers involved are very small and the results are complicated by changes in the nature of the alternatives available to people of different ages. The data indicate considerable stability between father and child in party preference in those cases in which the respondent knew the father's party preference, and even greater continuity if the left-right dichotomy rather than specific parties is examined (see table 15). The similarities are strong at the mass level and even stronger at the elite levels. Especially significant is the advantage that the Christian Democratic party gains from those who recalled that their fathers had no party preferences.

But the above comments refer to the 27 percent of the population who knew their father's party preferences. The portion is slightly higher among those under forty, since they grew up under the present regime and missed the confused party situation of their parents' formative years. Moreover, the overall picture is one of little discussion of politics in the family: Only 4 percent of the sample stated that their fathers discussed politics "often" during their youth, and an additional 17 percent replied "sometimes"; 75 percent said "never," and 4 percent did not answer. Moreover, only 3 percent stated that their fathers were "very much" interested in politics, and 4 percent said "moderately."

It seems clear that parents must not be the only sources of political

TABLE 15
Intergenerational Transfer of Partisan Preferences
(%)

RESPONDENT'S IDENTIFICATION

Father's Identification	PCI			PSIUP	PSI-PSDI			PRI	DC			PLI	MON	MSI
	Mass	Coun-cilor	Deputy	Mass	Mass	Coun-cilor	Deputy	Mass	Mass	Coun-cilor	Deputy	Mass	Mass	Mass
PCI	39	29	26	7	6	1	5	0	1	0	0	0	*	0
Socialist (all)	39	58	53	72	60	74	82	28	11	14	23	14	*	44
PRI	1	1	11	0	2	3	0	43	1	5	0	0	*	0
DC	6	4	5	7	18	10	5	7	57	54	58	33	*	16
PLI	1	0	0	7	3	3	5	7	3	5	4	33	*	20
MON	3	1	0	0	4	1	0	0	5	0	8	5	*	0
MSI or PNF (Fascist)	12	7	5	7	8	8	5	14	21	23	8	14	*	20
Total %	100	100	100	100	101	100	102	99	99	101	101	99	—	100
N	101	73	19	14	119	72	22	14	279	84	26	21	5	25

*Percentage not computed on fewer than 10 cases.

partisanship. Other influences are substantial, and we will now turn to an examination of several of the most important ones.

OTHER INFLUENCES ON THE TRANSMISSION OF PARTISANSHIP

While parent-child continuity in partisanship is impressive, the large majority of Italians who claim not to know their father's partisan preferences leads us to search for additional explanations for the perpetuation of the traditions. We are fortunate that this subject has been thoroughly analyzed by Sani using not only the data from our 1968 survey but also those from a 1972 survey conducted by Barnes and Sani.[20] This later survey contained questions for dealing with this analytical problem that were not asked in the 1968 study. Moreover, Sani has incorporated aggregate data that complement the two national surveys. In this section we will briefly summarize Sani's basic findings. Readers seeking greater detail should refer to the original article.[21] Sani examined the impact of primary groups, organizational networks, and community of residence. We will report on each of these in turn.

The primary groups examined are family, friends, and coworkers. The family is quite homogeneous politically. The families of 76 percent of the 1972 respondents were essentially similar in political preference, 11 percent were mixed, and only 13 percent were hostile to the political preferences of the respondent. Only 29 percent of the groups of friends and 22 percent of the coworkers had the same preferences.[22] Moreover, respondents claim to discuss politics more with work colleagues, who represent diverse views, than with family or friends. But far more attach influence to the opinions of the family (70 percent) than coworkers (16 percent) or friends (29 percent). Sani concludes that the social contexts that are "potentially more significant as vehicles of change are also the least effective as sources of influence."[23] And, of course, the work groups involve only the employed portion of the population, hence their impact is restricted. Primary groups thus serve to reinforce continuity in partisanship.

Our previous analyses have emphasized the importance of the organizational networks of the Church and of the left. The 1972 findings reported by Sani strongly support this emphasis. He found that about 35 percent of the voting-age population had at least one organizational affiliation. Many others have ties through the Church or through members of the family. Most of these ties are to the two major networks of the Church and of the left, and in 1972 less than 1 percent of the respondents reported ties with *both* major networks.

The political tradition of the community of residence is the final influence to be considered. Using the popular vote received by the Christian Democratic and the Socialist and Communist parties together in 1946 at the communal level, Sani has demonstrated the tenacity of early voting patterns.[24] Moreover, in areas of strength the parties receive more votes than would be expected on the basis of the socioeconomic characteristics of the communes. Sani found that the younger cohorts internalized political orientations in line with the traditions existing before they entered political life.[25] Other scholars have noted that pockets of opposition within the communes have a remarkable tenacity and have set limits on the expansion of the dominant tradition of the commune.[26]

To understand what keeps the tradition from overwhelming the minority in the commune, Sani examined the interrelationships of the various influences. He found the relationships to be weak; for example, homogeneous primary groups are not found disproportionately in communes dominated by one tradition. Those politically deviant from the point of view of the dominant tradition find reinforcement in their homogeneous families and their networks. In fact, organizational ties and church attendance—the two variables that we emphasize throughout this book—are more important than the tradition of the community.[27]

It is clear that there are several sources of the continuity of the traditions. Our measure probably underestimates the level of knowledge of father's preference, as respondents seem reluctant to delve deeply into family affairs, but even with our data the importance of family is clear. Equally apparent is the influence of other primary groups and of the networks. And, especially for those who lack clear cues from the primary groups and networks, the political tradition of the commune also exerts a strong influence.

6

Political Involvement

We have argued that a discussion of representation must encompass a consideration of mobilization as well, for the former is dependent on the latter: Representation is not meaningful without some sort of ties between the representative and the represented. And of course political mobilization means partisan involvement in the political system. The previous chapter has shown the predominant role of social networks in the mobilization of the population. The present chapter will examine the impact of variables that are more familiar to social scientists. We will concentrate on the mass sample. Elite partisan involvement in politics may vary, but compared with mass publics elites are linked closely to the political system. Mass publics, on the other hand, exhibit a range of partisan involvement from the most militant to those completely oblivious of the existence of politics.

LEVELS OF POLITICAL INVOLVEMENT
In our discussion of mobilization we distinguished several ways in which people are tied into the polity. At first glance these patterns may seem to form a developmental sequence, from clientelism through participation in democratically organized political parties. But we don't assume complete coincidence. While there may be developmental aspects of patterns of mobilization, we have already pointed out that clientelism can coexist with many forms of political organization and levels of economic development. Moreover, patterns of mobilization are systemic characteristics, not individual ones. That is, the nature of

the system itself is the primary determinant of *how* an individual is mobilized, of the patterns of ties that develop. But individual *levels* of involvement are not dependent on the developmental or other characteristics of systems; individual involvement can be high or low under any pattern of mobilization. In short, the level of political involvement is an individual characteristic, while patterns of political mobilization refer to the systemic level. While we will mention several aspects of mobilization in this discussion of political involvement, our subject matter in this section is the level rather than the pattern of mobilization.

The Nature of the Typology

To be useful, an approach to the study of political involvement must make sense theoretically and it must be operationalizable. Several scholars have discussed the conceptualization and measurement of political involvement. In *The Civic Culture*, Almond and Verba distinguished citizens, subjects, and parochials.[1] Citizens were those involved in the political input process by which decisions were made; subjects were only passively tied into the polity; parochials were not aware of being linked at all to the larger political system. Milbrath divides the population into "gladiators," "spectators," and "apathetics," categories that parallel those of Almond and Verba.[2] In *Participation in America*, Verba and Nie used a more complex typology that explicitly included modes as well as levels of participation.[3] Despite the absence of agreement on terminology, most typologies make similar distinctions among the activists, those passively involved, and those not involved at all, paralleling the citizen-subject-parochial division of Almond and Verba and the three-fold division of Milbrath.

The typology used in this chapter reflects these general subdivisions, but without the normative connotations of *The Civic Culture*'s labels and with some subdivisions that reflect the particular Italian situation. We distinguish five levels of involvement. "Party members" are a very important group in Italy. Most activists are party members, though it must be recognized that party membership is more important in some parties than in others. As there are many Italians who express verbal interest in politics, we have distinguished between the "Actively Interested" and the "Passively Interested." The former claim to have done something requiring activity, such as working for a party or candidate, attending rallies, making a financial contribution to a party (a rare activity in Italy), or trying to convince friends to vote as they do. The Passively Interested claim to be interested in politics in general or the electoral campaign, or both, but beyond making this claim do nothing more than vote. The "Vote Only" expressed no concern with politics beyond voting.

"Nonvoters" form the final category. Almost everyone votes, and our sample overrepresents voters, presumably because of embarrassment at admitting to a violation of the cultural norm. In operationalizing the Nonvoter category we were forced to include everyone who had not voted in every legislative election since becoming eligible. It is obvious that there are many reasons why one would miss voting in a particular election, such as illness or unavoidable absence from the precinct (there are no provisions for absentee voting in Italy), so we have obviously mixed together several types of nonvoters. We had to do this because only ten people claimed never to have voted since becoming eligible. Another fifty respondents claimed to have voted in "some" elections, and 100 respondents claimed to have voted in "most" elections. Even by lumping these three groups together we have only 160 (6.4 percent of the sample) in the Nonvoter category. For many purposes they could be grouped with the Vote Only category, were it not that nonvoting possesses a theoretical interest outweighing the inelegance that it brings to the typology.

Respondents were coded into the highest applicable level of involvement whether or not they had met all the requirements for lesser levels, so the scale does not meet Guttman criteria.

Party Differences in Involvement

The numerous differences among Italian parties in structure, relationships with members and voters, and role of the party organization have already been noted. Differences in the levels of involvement of their identifiers are likewise to be expected, and that is the case. The higher involvement of the followers of the PCI and MSI is immediately apparent (see table 16). Eighteen percent of the Communists and 17 percent of the Neofascists claim membership. On the other hand, followers of the secular center and right parties are most active in ways other than membership, as 21 percent of the Republicans, 26 percent of the Liberals, and 38 percent of the MSI are actively interested. Indeed, fully 55 percent of the latter fall into the two most active categories; the next most active are the Republicans, with 38 percent in the two highest categories, and the PCI, with 36 percent.

The incidence of those low in involvement among DC supporters is important, for the high turnout in Italian elections aids the DC and, to a lesser extent, the PCI. The DC is quite successful among people who

TABLE 16
Political Involvement, by Partisan Identification
(%)

PARTY

LEVEL OF INVOLVEMENT	PCI	PSIUP	PSI-PSDI	PRI	DC	PLI	MON	MSI
Nonvoter	5	6	5	0	5	1	21	0
Vote only	24	24	18	21	35	19	36	11
Passively interested	34	40	50	41	38	46	21	34
Actively interested	18	20	19	21	14	26	21	38
Party member	18	10	7	17	7	7	0	17
Total %	99	100	99	100	99	99	99	100
N	308	50	399	29	1,064	72	14	47

in many systems would be nonvoters; if only those who express some interest in politics voted, the electoral results would be much less favorable to the Christian Democratic party. The low level of involvement of Monarchist identifiers is also evident.

The relationship between involvement and strength of partisanship is the conventional one. Of the Party Members, 78 percent felt "very close" to their party and 20 percent felt "more or less close." For the Actively Interested the figures were 43 percent and 43 percent; for the Passively Interested, 26 percent and 55 percent; for the Vote Only, 29 percent and 37 percent; and for the Nonvoters, 29 percent and 45 percent. While the first two categories of involvement follow linear expectations, the lower three are rather similar to one another.

Sex Differences

Sex is strongly related to involvement. Women provide 60 percent of the Nonvoters, 67 percent of the Vote Only, 48 percent of the Passively Interested, 32 percent of the Actively Interested, and only 25 percent of the Party Members.

There are several reasons for this. It should be recalled that women were enfranchised at the national level in Italy only after the Second World War. Following the logic of the model of the development of partisanship elaborated by Converse in "Of Time and Partisan Stability," and which we discussed in Chapter 5, we would expect older women to be less deeply involved.[4]

Moreover, we expect the logic of this model to apply to all kinds of involvement and not just the development of a partisan attachment. Indeed, we believe that in the Italian case it should be even more useful for involvement in general than for partisanship in particular.

This is because many people acquire a strong sense of the direction—and sometimes the intensity—of partisan preference through their network ties. As a result, their political partisanship is only in part politically motivated, even though it has immense implications for partisanship and the party system. Thus we would expect the involvement of women to be low compared with men, and this is indeed the case (see table 17).

TABLE 17
Involvement and Partisanship by Sex
(%)

INVOLVEMENT	SEX	PARTY							
		PCI	PSIUP	PSI-PSDI	PRI	DC	PLI	MON	MSI
Nonvoter	F	5	13	7	0	6	3	27	0
	M	6	3	4	0	4	0	*	0
Vote only	F	38	40	27	44	42	39	27	7
	M	14	17	14	10	23	5	*	12
Passively	F	31	47	54	33	37	35	27	43
interested	M	37	37	49	45	40	54	*	30
Actively	F	15	0	10	22	10	23	18	43
interested	M	20	29	24	20	20	29	*	36
Party member	F	11	0	2	0	4	0	0	7
	M	23	14	9	25	12	12	*	21
Total N	F	122	15	134	9	664	31	11	14
	M	186	35	265	20	400	41	3	33

*Fewer than 5 cases.

Age Differences

Political involvement generally follows a seemingly universal life-cycle pattern, with the young busy with other activities until their late thirties, at which time political activity increases moderately until about age sixty, after which it declines slowly.[5] This seems not to be strictly applicable to Italy, at least for many dimensions of politics. Age has only the slightest impact on the level of involvement of the population as a whole, though the age curve tends to follow the pattern just described. This is true whether we examine sex differences (see fig. 2) or left-center-right differences (see fig. 3). The Converse model discussed

FIGURE 2

Mean Differences in Political Involvement by Age and Sex

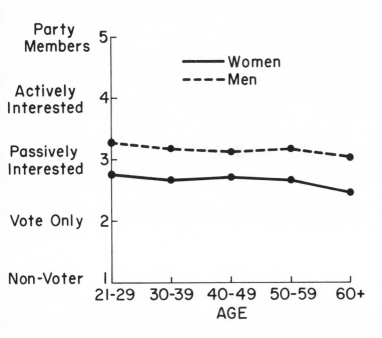

above led us to anticipate wide differences between older men and women, with these differences narrowing and perhaps disappearing among those socialized entirely during the republican period. But this is obviously not the case. The spread between men and women in level of involvement remains relatively constant across all age cohorts.

Despite the relative absence of differences associated with age, the sex differences among the old carry political consequences as a result of the greater life expectancy of women. According to our data, the DC received 77 percent of the votes of women sixty and over in 1968, while receiving only 62 percent from those under sixty. In the 1961 census there were 3,050,287 men and 3,996,150 women of age sixty and over, giving an excess of 945,863 women over men in that age category.

FIGURE 3

Mean Differences in Political Involvement by Age and Political Tendency

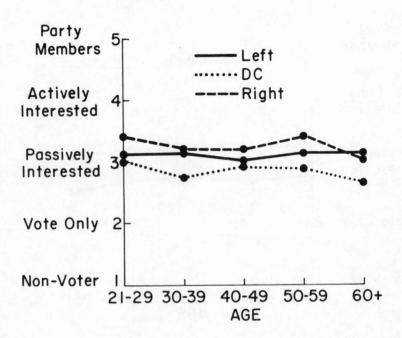

Party
Members

Actively
Interested

Passively
Interested

Vote Only

Non-Voter

21-29 30-39 40-49 50-59 60+

AGE

Left
DC
Right

Geographical Area

Area is a variable that illustrates our contention that patterns of mobilization relate to the system and not to the individual, for we quickly learn that southerners are more highly involved in politics than other Italians, while those from the industrialized northwest and north central areas are least likely to be highly involved. Each of the three southern areas outranks all nonsouthern areas in the higher two involvement categories in every instance. In the three northern areas, the Passively Interested category predominates. Table 18 demonstrates these differences quite clearly and reinforces findings that show that politics is more important in the south than in other areas. And this is in spite of the fact that southerners rank lower on most of the variables associated with high involvement, such as high occupational status, education,

TABLE 18
Political Involvement by Geographical Area
(%)

INVOLVEMENT					AREA			
	Total	North West	North Center	North East	Center	South West	South East	Islands
Nonvoters	5	4	2	4	5	10	4	6
Vote only	31	35	28	27	32	32	34	31
Passively interested	41	49	60	50	39	24	28	31
Actively interested	16	9	6	11	18	27	20	21
Party members	7	4	3	8	6	8	13	10
Total %	100	101	99	100	100	101	99	99
N	2,426	269	347	459	461	345	238	307

and urbanization. Politics in the south is more highly personalized than in other areas, and this is true of all of the parties. It is much more likely to involve face-to-face contacts and personal activity and is less dependent on the mass media and other forms of impersonal channels of communication. The personalism of the parties and the relative weakness of secondary associations lead to a frantic search for preference votes by the candidates, and this, too, seems to increase involvement. Politics is also simply very important to people in the south, for it is the chief determinant of the quality of their lives. And it is all of these factors, rather than the usual socioeconomic ones, that are conducive to higher participation in the south.

Occupational Status

There is widespread evidence that people in higher occupational categories are more involved than others, and this is generally true in Italy as well. Although white-collar respondents are more involved than blue-collar, this is not true at the higher levels of involvement: There is no difference between white-collar and blue-collar occupations in levels of party membership (see table 19). On the other hand, a higher percentage of blue-collar respondents are found in the Vote Only category. Furthermore, occupational status differences are similar in the north and south, even though the overall levels of involvement differ.

Education

Education generally follows the universal pattern of increasing education being associated with increasing political involvement. Educational differences are small at higher levels of involvement. The impact

TABLE 19
Political Involvement and Occupational Status
(%)

INVOLVEMENT	OCCUPATIONAL STATUS	
	White Collar	Blue Collar
Nonvoter	4	5
Vote only	19	37
Passively interested	49	37
Actively interested	21	13
Party member	7	7
Total %	100	99
N	911	1,484

of education is more obvious at the lower levels: 74 percent of those with no formal education and 40 percent of those with only elementary schooling fall in the lowest two levels of involvement. The importance of these differences is magnified by the fact that 6 percent of the respondents had no formal education and 69 percent attended elementary school only. Table 20 summarizes the uncontrolled relationship between education and involvement.

TABLE 20
Political Involvement and Education
(%)
FORMAL EDUCATION

INVOLVEMENT	None	Elementary	Lower Middle	Technical	Liceo	Some University	University Graduate
Nonvoters	8	5	4	2	2	4	2
Vote only	66	35	16	8	9	11	4
Passively interested	12	39	52	53	58	38	61
Actively interested	10	13	19	27	25	38	29
Party members	5	7	9	11	5	9	4
Total %	101	99	100	101	99	100	100
N	152	1,660	281	157	55	66	49

NOTE: Gamma = .39.

These relationships remain similar in structure but altered in strength when simple controls are introduced. Thus the overall relationship is Gamma=.39. But for the north and center combined it is Gamma=.44, while for the south it is .33. And education is much more strongly related to involvement for women (Gamma=.45) than for men (.29). Among party members the relationships are reversed; a smaller proportion of men with at least some university belongs to a party than is true of those with lesser education, while among women the highest portion of party members is found in the highest education category. In fact, the percentage of women who are party members is greater than that of men among respondents with some university education. As is so often the case, education seems to be a principal method for women to break with traditional cultural patterns. We have already noted that education beyond the elementary level is associated with weakened support for the DC. The increasing education of women has the same implications. Thus a continuing rise in educational levels has immense implications for the party system.

Sizes of Communes

Size of commune is a good measure of urbanization, and we find that there is a slight rise in mean political involvement as size of commune increases (see table 21). This rise is due largely to a decline in the Vote Only category and an increase in those Passively Interested, undoubtedly reflecting the greater number of stimuli in larger communes.

TABLE 21
Political Involvement and Size of Commune
(%)

SIZE OF COMMUNE

INVOLVEMENT	Up to 5,000	5,001– 20,000	20,001– 50,000	50,001– 200,000	200,001 and Above
Nonvoter	5	4	5	7	4
Vote only	35	35	31	25	22
Passively interested	35	38	40	46	54
Actively interested	18	16	16	12	16
Party member	8	7	8	10	5
Total %	101	100	100	100	101
N	540	809	440	297	340

NETWORK TIES AND POLITICAL INVOLVEMENT

The importance for partisanship of ties with social networks has been demonstrated. These ties are equally significant for political involvement, and they demonstrate dramatically the differences between the left and Church networks in involvement. The numbers tied into the Church networks are greater than the left, but the latter are far more involved than the former; when combined with the severe underrepresentation of the Communists in our sample this finding goes far toward explaining why the left segment of the population seems more active than the Catholic: it is.

It is not difficult to see why this is so. The left network—as we have operationalized it—operates through a trade union, while church attendance is the measure of the network for the Church. The former is much more directly political than the latter. However, this distinction does not explain why members of the Catholic CISL are so much less involved than members of the left CGIL (see table 22). The differences are quite substantial. Moreover, left union members are more involved than those of the "other" category. Respondents who are members of no union are lowest in levels of involvement. While we have emphasized the higher end of the involvement index, it is equally impor-

TABLE 22
Political Involvement, by Union Ties
(%)

	UNION TIES			
INVOLVEMENT	Left-CGIL	Catholic-CISL	Other	None
Nonvoter	2	6	3	5
Vote only	11	15	20	35
Passively interested	35	48	46	40
Actively interested	28	19	20	14
Party members	25	12	10	5
Total %	101	100	99	99
N	161	118	292	1,929

tant that union members fall into the lower two categories much less often than nonmembers.

The higher level of involvement of respondents in the left network is also apparent in the relationship between church attendance and involvement. Those who claim to attend church weekly overwhelmingly support parties of the center and right; they are much less involved than those who attend less frequently, while those who never attend are the most involved (see table 23).

These findings suggest that the networks of the left and of the Church involve people in quite different ways. The left has much higher mass levels of involvement; but in our sample the Church network is larger, even taking into account the underrepresentation of the Communists. And Nonvoters are not concentrated in any particular category. Thus

TABLE 23
Political Involvement, by Church Attendance
(%)

	ATTENDANCE				
INVOLVEMENT	Weekly	Often	Sometimes	Rarely	Never
Nonvoter	5	5	4	6	7
Vote only	34	28	28	26	26
Passively interested	42	44	42	36	31
Actively interested	14	16	17	20	20
Party members	5	7	8	11	16
Total %	100	100	99	99	100
N	1,196	482	431	231	152

the Church network does an adequate job in getting out the vote, even if it does not encourage higher levels of involvement. Furthermore, this low involvement may render its leadership task easier, for the fragmented DC would have an even more difficult time maintaining its unity if its supporters were as active as those of the left. In addition, the fact that Church networks are not primarily political reduces even more the stresses on the DC, as it restricts bargaining to a sector of the party and network elite. Whether this is good for Italian democracy is another question.

PSYCHOLOGICAL MEASURES AND POLITICAL INVOLVEMENT
The existence of a relationship between psychological measures and various indicators of political involvement has been demonstrated in many studies undertaken over a considerable period of time in several cultures. These studies suggest that high levels of involvement are usually associated with high scores on measures of efficacy, trust, confidence, and so on. These individual level characteristics have been demonstrated to be especially important in the United States and several other countries. Milbrath, citing many studies, concluded that "persons who feel efficacious politically are much more likely to become actively involved in politics."[6]

There are reasons for questioning the universality of these relationships. In all societies, structural factors intervene between the individual and involvement in the political system, and these may facilitate or hinder the involvement of particular groups.[7] The importance of these structural factors in totalitarian mobilization systems can be easily understood: People are mobilized politically regardless of their personal characteristics, and where mobilization is selective the criteria are more likely to be social (class, race, and so on) than psychological.

Because of the high turnout in Italy, there is little variance to be explained, so the absence of a strong relationship between voting and psychological characteristics is not surprising. But the relationship between these characteristics and other forms of involvement is likewise weak. Before demonstrating this we must introduce our measurements.

The Measurement of Trust, Political Efficacy, and Personal Efficacy
Our study contained eight measures selected to reflect the respondent's underlying attitudes toward the self and others. In other studies these had formed several scales. Since they had not been validated for Italy we performed a factor analysis on the eight items to determine if they tapped the same underlying dimensions in Italy as elsewhere. We found that they did, so we constructed three different scales, using the items that loaded heavily on each factor.

The first scale measures *political trust*. We dichotomized the responses to the following questions, in each case separating the most extreme answer from the others:

1. "Some people think that many people in government aren't very honest. Do you think there are many like this, only some, or almost none?"
2. "Do you think that people in government waste the revenues from our taxes?"
3. "Up to what point, in your opinion, can one have confidence that those who govern us act as they ought?"

For this scale we had complete data for 1,908 of the 2,500 respondents. With four scores possible on the scale, 39 percent of those included were in the most trusting category, 28 percent in the next, 14 percent in the third, and 19 percent in the least trusting category.

The second scale measures *sense of political efficacy*. It was constructed in a similar fashion from the following questions:

1. "I don't think that the government worries much about what people like me think."
2. "Politics and government sometimes seem so complicated that people like me can't really understand what's going on."
3. "In general, the deputies we elect quickly lose contact with the people."

It has complete data for 2,125 respondents. The most efficacious category contains 13 percent of the reduced sample, the second contains 17 percent, the third 24 percent, and the least efficacious category 46 percent.

The third scale measures *sense of personal efficacy*. It was created from the following questions:

1. "In general, would you say that you can trust other people or, on the contrary, would you say that you can never take enough precautions with some people?"
2. "In general, in your opinion, which reputation is preferable: the reputation of knowing how to work with other people, or the reputation of knowing how to get out of jams yourself?"

We have complete data on only 1,661 of the 2,500 respondents. The most efficacious category contains 26 percent of the reduced samples, the middle one 17 percent, and the least efficacious set 56 percent.

Psychological Indicators and Political Involvement

None of the three psychological indicators is highly associated with political involvement. Trust has no impact whatsoever. Political efficacy and personal efficacy are very weakly associated (see table 24). Furthermore, the controls used previously in this chapter make no difference on relationships.

For example, relationships are the same for men and women, and even the percentage in each of the five trust levels is similar. Gamma for men is .00 and for women −.05 for the relationship between trust and involvement. For political efficacy the relationship with involvement is Gamma = −.17 for men and −.02 for women. For personal efficacy the Gammas are −.23 for men and −.19 for women. North-south differences are even smaller. For the north the relationship between trust and involvement is −.04, while for the south it is −.02. On the other two measures the Gammas are identical for north and south. Finally, using subjective social class as the indicator, the relationships are similar within the working class and the middle class. For trust the former is Gamma of .00 and the latter .01; for political efficacy they are −.17 and −.14; for personal efficacy, −.20 and −.18.

These weak relationships between political involvement and our psychological indicators have several possible interpretations. At least two of them merit exploration, though we are not able to choose between them; in fact, we consider them complementary rather than conflicting. We will label one of these interpretations the cognitive, the other the structural.

The cognitive interpretation assumes that Italians who are involved

TABLE 24
Psychological Indicators and Political Involvement
(%)

POLITICAL INVOLVEMENT	POLITICAL TRUST				POLITICAL EFFICACY				PERSONAL EFFICACY		
	High 1	2	3	Low 4	High 1	2	3	Low 4	High 1	2	Low 3
Non-voters	4	4	5	6	4	2	4	6	3	4	6
Vote only	20	25	27	26	12	29	25	30	18	21	32
Passively interested	49	45	46	33	44	41	45	43	48	41	40
Actively interested	18	17	15	24	26	16	18	16	19	23	17
Party members	8	9	8	11	14	11	8	5	12	11	6
Total %	99	100	101	100	100	99	100	100	100	100	101
	Gamma = −.02				Gamma = −.19				Gamma = −.22		

in political activity are especially aware of the inadequacies in the performance of the authorities of their political system. Our questions were formulated for American mass publics, where it is assumed, for good reason, that those higher in political involvement view the system more positively than those lower. Furthermore, in the United States those who exhibit low efficacy, trust, and so on, were thought to do so because of personal psychological characteristics. But it is quite possible for lack of trust and efficacy to reflect well-founded cognitive evaluations of the political system. Involved Italians are much more likely than the uninvolved to be aware of the gap between expectations and reality, and they are much more likely to see this gap in partisan terms. Hence, unlike in the American polity, those low on trust and efficacy are apt to continue partisan activity to change the situation rather than to withdraw into apathy. In our opinion, for an indeterminate number of Italians low scores on trust and efficacy reflect a conscious cognitive evaluation of the system rather than their unconscious psychological predispositions.

The structural interpretation reaches the same conclusion by a different path. It suggests that involvement in Italian politics is greatly affected by one's location in the networks of the traditions and hence is relatively independent of individual psychological characteristics. Network involvement facilitates political involvement; those who would be apathetic in other systems may be mobilized by the networks. Indeed, Italian involvement depends much less on the "self-starter" phenomenon common in the United States and more on closeness to the institutions of the traditions.

These findings leave us with somewhat of a puzzle as to the utility of these psychological measures in comparative politics. We have demonstrated that they tap the same underlying dimensions as in the United States, and they seem to have similar interpretations in meaning. Yet, they relate differently to involvement and probably to other variables as well. Thus once again we are alerted to the truism that great caution is called for in the application in other countries of concepts and measures developed in a single country. The absence of a strong relationship between involvement and psychological indicators is dramatic substantiation of this need for caution.

POLITICAL KNOWLEDGE AND POLITICAL INVOLVEMENT

Knowledge about politics is of course an individual level characteristic, but it is not what we usually mean by a "psychological" indicator. Previous research on PSI members by Barnes indicates that political knowledge is related to both education and involvement.[8] That is, high knowledge levels are found among those who rank high on both. Participation in party activities can substitute for education as a source of political knowledge for the poorly educated. Even so, at any level of participation the poorly educated score lower on measures of knowledge. In this section we will test these conclusions on a national sample.

We have used two measures of political knowledge that seem especially appropriate for the study of representation. These are the respondents' ability to recall without prompting or to recognize when presented with a list the names of the political parties in the electoral campaign of 1968, and the respondents' ability to recall the names and party affiliations of candidates running in their constituencies during that campaign.

Knowledge of Party Names

We find the expected relationship between the level of involvement and ability to recognize the parties. Gamma is .38; the percentage naming the eight major parties ranges from 14 percent in the Nonvoter and 8 percent in the Vote Only, to 25 percent in the Passively Involved, 35 percent in the Actively Involved, and 50 percent among Party Members. The median response was four parties in the Nonvoter, three in the Vote Only, five in the Passively Involved, six in the Actively Involved, and eight among Party Members.

Education is even more strongly related to recognition of party names. Gamma is .49; only 15 percent of those with elementary education, 40 percent of those with more than five years through high school, and 67 percent of those who had attended a university could recognize all eight parties. When the two variables are combined, it is clear that involvement is equally important for all education levels, as the Gamma relationships between involvement and knowledge of party names are similar within education levels (.34; .33; .31).

Knowledge of Candidates

We performed a similar analysis with the respondents' ability to recall the names and party affiliation of candidates in their constituency. We coded no more than three candidates and their parties, regardless of how many were named or how many were on the ballot in the constituency. Only 11 percent of the respondents named at least three of each, even though in 1968 all voters were permitted three preference votes and those in the larger constituencies were allowed four; 57 percent could not or would not name any candidate and party.

The patterns by level of involvement and education are the expected ones. Among Nonvoters 7 percent were in the top category; among Voters Only, 5 percent; Passively Involved, 9 percent; Actively Involved, 19 percent; and among Party Members 30 percent were in the top category. Gamma is .34 for involvement and knowledge. For education and knowledge, Gamma is .26; and 9 percent in the lowest education category, 16 percent in the middle, and 23 percent in the highest knew at least three names and parties. When the relationship is examined within educational categories, involvement is clearly demonstrated to be more important for those with low and middle levels of education (Gamma =.19 and .17) than for high (-.08). But these relationships are all weak.

It is of interest that education is related more strongly than involvement to the ability to recognize parties, while for candidates' names and affiliations involvement is more important. This undoubtedly reflects the more personalized aspect of the latter. Moreover, when we look at relationships within the party grouping of left, center (DC), and right, we find the relationships between involvement and candidate knowledge much weaker on the right (Gamma for left =.34; DC=.37; right=.19) and nonexistent for the relationship between education and knowledge (Gamma for left=.30; DC=.27; right=.00). This reinforces our contention that the right is much more personalistic and probably more clientelistic than the left and center.

Several conclusions emerge from this analysis of political involvement. The importance of the networks is evident, as is the greater success of the left network in involving its supporters in political activities. The absence of a strong relationship between involvement and several measures of a psychological nature also stands out. Finally, our measures of political knowledge demonstrate that the parties of the right are more personalistic than those of the left and center, though it is unclear whether this is due to the smaller and hence more intimate nature of the former, the higher socio-economic levels of their followers, or other causes.

The weak impact of individual psychological characteristics is especially striking. This finding demonstrates that system level phenomena are as important as characteristics of the individual in understanding levels of involvement in political systems. Ties with the networks of the left and of the Church are not dependent on individual politicization. The weak relationship between involvement and the psychological measures suggests the need for caution in the transfer of theory and measurement from one culture to another. For these measures function as well in Italy as in the United States, the country in which they were developed, at least in the methodological sense that they seem to tap the same underlying dimensions of orientations toward politics. However, they function in a different institutional setting, and hence their consequences for the political system are different.

7

Attitudes—Left and Right

We have already explored differences among Italian parties in the social characteristics of their electorates. It is not surprising that these differences are accompanied by corresponding differences in political perceptions, including self-locations in political space. For the Italian electorate views politics on a left-right dimension: almost 80 percent of the respondents were able to locate the Christian Democratic party on the left-right dimension, and only slightly fewer could similarly locate the PCI.

In this chapter we will examine the utility of a spatial model for simplifying the structure of Italian political perceptions. We will demonstrate that left-right self-placement fits amazingly well with attitudes toward major issues.

SPATIAL MODELS AND ITALIAN POLITICS

It is commonplace for scholars, politicians, journalists, and others to analyze politics in spatial terms. The assumption that political objects can be located at a particular point in a space that extends from left to right has long been current in the idiom of politics. It is not at all strange that the terms "left" and "right" should be especially relevant in Italy, for Italian parties, policies, politicians, and voters seem to fit neatly on a single left-right dimension. Multidimensionality, which often complicates spatial models, is not a great problem. The socioeconomic, religious, and foreign-policy dimensions of Italian politics turn out to be mutually reinforcing. At least this is the conventional wisdom. Before subjecting this contention to closer scrutiny a discussion of the background of the argument is needed.

In the search for elegance and parsimony in models of political behavior, students of politics have increasingly turned to the other social sciences. One promising model of political processes is derived from the analysis of optimum location of economic enterprises. Deriving from Hotelling[1] and refined by Smithies,[2] it has been applied to mass and elite democratic political behavior by Downs.[3]

The model demonstrated that the optimum location of an enterprise in relation to markets and to competitors would place competing firms near one another. The familiar analogy is that Woolworth's and Kresge's are near one another rather than at opposite ends of Main Street. In an inelastic market, each would recruit customers from its hinterland; there would be no likelihood of anyone passing by one store to shop at one further away, for location would ensure lower costs for customers nearer in space.

It is the merit of Downs that he has worked out the implications of this for party competition.[4] Central to Downs's argument is the assumption that political parties seek office by adopting policies that will attract a maximum number of voters. These voters are strung out along a continuum that reaches from left to right. For Downs, the relevant dimension is the extent of governmental intervention in the economy. The distribution of voters on that continuum reflects their attitudes toward that dimension and dictates the strategies that parties employ to seek votes. Logically it also determines the number of parties that exist in the system. The common bell-shaped curve distribution of voters, for example, encourages a two-party system, with the policies of the two converging and even overlapping in order to attract the voters in the center. A bimodal system, on the other hand, suggests a different type of two-party system, one that is highly polarized and with few shared policy preferences. A bimodal or multimodal system might logically lead to a multiparty system. As the curve becomes flatter, fewer people would be occupying an equivalent segment, and the difficulty of reconciling the policy needs of the different segments would increase. This would encourage the proliferation of parties to appeal to particular segments of the distribution. Rather than the converging policy preferences in a two-party system, multiparty systems encourage sharp differentiation of policies between parties adjacent on the continuum.

Additional discussion of the general patterns of relationships between party systems and the distribution of opinions would carry us far afield from our present subject, which is the particular pattern in Italy rather than a critique of spatial models in general. However, several important theoretical questions should be noted. One concerns the nature of the space of the left-right continuum. What does it contain? Is it viewed similarly by elites and mass? Do different political groups agree on its composition? Insofar as they relate to spatial models in general these questions need not concern us. Yet it is necessary to specify what the space refers to in this chapter. Downs labeled the space "ideology," which is not the same thing as to define it. His emphasis was on a single dimension, that of the degree of governmental intervention in the economy. He seems to use this example as a shorthand for sets of policy preferences and political orientations consisting of elements that somehow hang together. He does not deal with the interesting question of why they hang together. We will deal with the left-right continuum as it was operationalized in the study—that is, as a scale on which respondents were asked to place themselves and the parties of the Italian system. Unlike Downs's reference to the desired degree of government intervention in the economy, our left-right dimension is open in meaning, with only the respondent (if anyone) knowing precisely what dimension was intended.[5]

However, we must note several problems of the model that derive from assumptions concerning the nature of the space. These have been analyzed by Stokes as the axioms of unidimensionality, fixed structure, ordered dimensions, and common reference.[6] He notes that the unreality of these axioms as applied to actual polities greatly weakens the appeal of spatial models. It is our thesis that the axioms do not greatly distort the reality of Italian politics. A short discussion will clarify the meaning and limitations of the thesis.

The axiom of unidimensionality posits that a single dimension dominates the politics of the polity. For Downs this was the degree of governmental intervention in the economy. As Stokes has pointed out, other dimensions quite often have been widely viewed as more important, and in all polities there is some degree of disagreement as to what constitutes the crucial issues. Religious cleavages have often been as important as economic ones, for example, and there is no logical or empirical reason for assuming that the distribution of opinions on one of these dimensions parallels that on the other. As dimensions are added, the number of possible combinations of opinions increases rapidly, and there could be a party to represent each possible combination of opinions. In practice, not every combination is equally likely to require recognition, but extant systems illustrate the very large number of parties that can be generated by a multidimensional politics.

The Italian polity is certainly a case in point. Italians are divided along the socioeconomic, religious, and foreign-policy dimensions, plus numerous less salient ones. However, the multiple cleavages do not cancel out a strong overall relationship between left-right position and party identification. One reason is that the large parties are essentially consistent on the three major dimensions. That is, the Communists tend to be redistributive, anticlerical, and anti-American, while the Christian Democrats are less redistributive, more clerical, and pro-American. Another reason is that those Italian parties that do not fit so neatly into this spatial model have few supporters compared with the mass parties that do conform to its expectations. Finally, the determining dimensions for voters may in reality be only a subset of those current in political debate. The inquiry into why the existence of multiple dimensions is compatible with a single left-right continuum will be taken up again later.

The axiom of fixed structure suggests that the definition of the space remains unchanged. Political reality, however, certainly is not fixed; issues change, parties surge and decline, political fads come and go. We cannot deal with the question of changes in Italian politics, as our data derive from a single study conducted at a particular moment in time. Although we do have information about prior voting preferences, the study of political change lies outside the scope of this book. But when an analysis of voting change in Italy is eventually concluded, it will probably demonstrate considerable stability in individual voting habits in the twenty years preceding this election in 1968. Thus, some 80 percent of the 1968 electorate claimed to have always voted for the same party. Considering only the electoral returns, which may, of course, be misleading, losses and gains of each party are quite small from election to election. Earlier elections, especially that of 1948, were conducted on the issue of God against communism. Recent elections have been more prosaic affairs, at least as compared with 1948. It is our hunch that the political attitudes of the individual Italian voter have changed very slightly and only quite slowly in the past few years.[7] This is a comment about the past; it is certainly not a prediction of future patterns.

The third axiom, that of ordered dimensions, posits that the parties can be ranked according to their stand on issues. Stokes, following Kurt Lewin, distinguishes between "valence issues," which "merely involve the linking of the parties with some condition that is positively or negatively valued by the electorate," and position issues.[8] Thus valence issues would not fit the spatial scheme, as all of the parties might in fact take the same position. Honesty in government, for example, is not likely to be the monopoly of a single party platform; it might, however, be the determining factor in an individual's vote because he feels that one party would in fact act with more integrity than another. In the Italian case we uncovered several valence issues, such as economic development of Italy, improvement of schools, and governmental stability. Analysis indicates that attitudes toward these issues are not as closely linked with partisan identification as are attitudes toward position issues on socioeconomic, religious, and foreign-policy questions. The evidence seems clear that in the Italian case in 1968, position rather than valence issues were determining. Again, we must enter the caveat that we are discussing a single election.

The final axiom is that of common reference, the possession of agreement between elites and mass as to the alternatives of governmental action. More than the other three, this is a question of degree. It is obvious that elite and mass do not view the system in exactly the same way anywhere. It seems equally clear that there is substantial congruence between the policy preferences of mass publics and elites in Italy, though it may be due as much to organizational and socialization variables as to ideology. The differences between Communist elites and voters, for example, are considerable on a number of dimensions, and the same can be said of the Christian Democrats. It is less certain that any profound political consequences flow from these differences. It is doubtful that complete agreement would make much difference for the political system, though it might alter the mobilization styles of elites if it were somehow to be achieved.

As this is a single study at a particular time, there is little that we can say about the problem of fixed structure or change in the definition of the space. Consequently, we will concentrate on the problems of unidimensionality, ordered dimensions, and common elite-mass references. First, the overall results will be presented.

THE ITALIAN ELECTORATE: LEFT AND RIGHT

It is the perceptions of mass publics rather than of elites that complicate most attempts to construct left-right models of party competition. Although mass publics may not seem to be clearly aware of left-right dimensions, it is seldom difficult for knowledgeable observers to detect meaningful gradations among parties along numerous dimensions. Hence we will begin with the more difficult case—the mass public.

It is not difficult for voters to think in left-right terms in the homeland of the world's largest nonruling Communist party—the symbol par excellence of the left—as well as the cradle of three potent symbols of the twentieth-century right—the Catholic church, the joint stock company, and fascism. Italy's history seems to encourage left-right thinking. Patterns of social stratification and the resulting elitism have exacerbated cleavages originating in both agricultural and industrial societies, and their historical legacies are a body politic sharply divided by ideology and social class. The early dominance of the country by the Liberals, the rise of Marxist socialism and its subsequent fragmentation, the mobilization of Catholics into a mass party that in part transcends class dimensions, and the survival of Fascist sympathies gave rise to parties holding the present loyalties of more than 95 percent of the voters. The result is that most Italian voters identify three blocs—the left, right, and Catholic, the last being in fact, as we will see, a center bloc.

Italian political mores and the professional ethics of the interviewers in 1968 precluded asking respondents how they voted in the previous election. Instead, respondents were asked, "To which party do you habitually feel closest?" plus questions dealing with consistency of voting, past voting behavior, closeness to party, and so on. As almost 80 percent claimed to have always voted for the same party, the fit between party identification and vote must be very close; but, given the uncertainties associated with recalled behavior, it should not be assumed.

The elites referred to in this section of the chapter are the municipal councilors only, as the left-right scale was not administered to the deputies. Pretests indicated that the latter found the simplicity and crudeness of the measure distasteful.

There would be virtually no disagreement among observers of Italian politics on the ranking of parties in table 25; and, as we shall see, the mass and elites concur. In order to tap perceptions of the parties on the left-right continuum we asked respondents to place parties that they had previously been able to identify on a scale from the extreme left to the extreme right (that is, zero to 100). We also asked them to place themselves on the scale. Of the total voter sample, 76 percent were able to place themselves on the left-right continuum; the portion ranged from a maximum of 97 percent for the PLI identifiers to a low of 79 percent for the DC. Only 47 percent of the nonidentifiers could locate themselves on the scale. There are many confirmations of the fit between left-right placement and party identification. The ranking of the parties is similar to their placement by expert opinion, though it

TABLE 25
Left-Right Placement of Italian Parties and Respondents
(0–100)

MASS

PARTY	By All Parties	N	By Identifiers of That Party Only	N	Self-Location of Party Identifiers	N
PCI	12.4	1,958	15.8	235	17.7	231
PSIUP	16.8	1,650	16.8	44	19.8	44
PSI-PSDI	32.7	1,875	33.1	284	34.9	283
PRI	51.1	1,688	44.8	27	44.4	27
DC	55.3	1,990	55.0	837	53.6	842
PLI	72.1	1,739	70.6	48	69.1	54
MON	74.8	1,600	65.8	12	64.2	12
MSI	78.0	1,744	76.7	42	77.1	41
Nonidentifiers	—	—	—	—	45.9	239

ELITE

PARTY	By All Elites	N	By Elites of That Party Only	N	Self-Location of Party Elites	N
PCI	10.2	383	9.3	117	10.6	102
PSIUP	10.3	379	—	—	—	—
PSI-PSDI	34.1	384	29.2	123	28.8	112
PRI	43.6	379	—	—	—	—
DC	52.8	384	46.3	144	43.9	129
PLI	79.8	382	—	—	—	—
MON	85.9	375	—	—	—	—
MSI	92.5	380	—	—	—	—
Nonidentifiers	—	—	—	—	—	—

has been achieved by respondents of a country with a low level of formal education at the mass level and little claimed interest in politics. The overall elite ranking is similar to the overall mass ranking, though the numbers assigned the parties differ somewhat, especially on the right. This is in part due to the weight of the Socialists and Communists in the elite ranking and to the absence of right-wing councilors in the elite sample. The overall relationship between left-right self-placement and party identification at the mass level is very strong: Gamma is .77. The relationship is also clear in the percentage of each party's identifiers that places itself between zero and 49 on the left-right scale. These are as follows: PCI, 87; PSIUP, 91; PSI-PSDI, 84; PRI, 44; DC, 14; PLI, 5; MON, 17 (only two respondents!); and MSI, 2.

Examination of the distribution of the mass electorate will help to redefine our understanding of several aspects of the Italian system. Figure 4 shows the overall distribution of left-right self-placement and the distribution of the individual parties. The most striking observation is the strong resemblance between the Christian Democratic distribution and that of the mass sample as a whole (see fig. 4). Of course, the sample somewhat overrepresents the DC and underrepresents the PCI and right. Undoubtedly a better sample would reveal a somewhat stronger right and a considerably stronger extreme left, not to mention a less exaggerated center. However, the general shape of the area under the curve would probably not change greatly. The DC dominates the area in which the bulk of the electorate is to be found, which is not surprising considering that the party has ruled for a quarter century.

It is also clear that the Italian electorate in 1968 was skewed to the left. The center-left formula thus certainly seemed to reflect the distribution of opinion. The right, though well represented in parties, is weak in numbers. But its existence is a prerequisite for the center position of the DC. The Italian system does not appear to be highly polarized in left-right terms, perhaps because the mass electorate's perception of the location of the three right-wing parties existing in 1968 caused the DC to be viewed as a center party. If the composition of the space were to change, if the perspective were to be foreshortened by the elimination of the right, so to speak, then the DC might be viewed in quite different terms. Perhaps the same change could result from the emergence of a new force on the extreme left, one that would disrupt the current hold of the PCI on that position and push that party toward the center. But this is speculation. The historical memory of fascism, the existence of a Neofascist party and other clearly

FIGURE 4
Left-Right Self-Placement

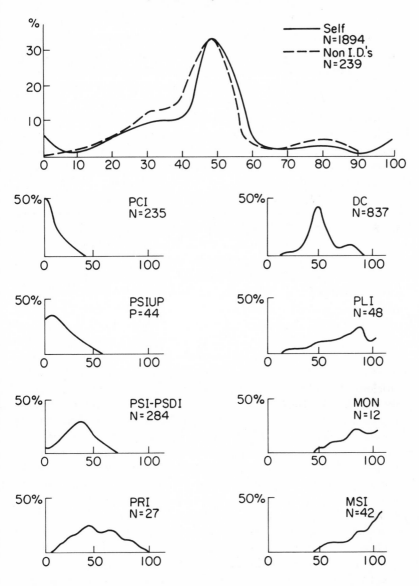

conservative parties, and perhaps other forces not yet isolated and analyzed placed the DC squarely in the center in 1968. In terms of the

105

distribution of left-right perspectives at that time, the center-left formula seemed attuned to political realities.

DIMENSIONS OF PUBLIC POLICY

We have shown that the political space of the Italian electorate is highly structured. Respondents are able to locate themselves on a left-right continuum, and they agree on the location of the parties as well. This generalized structuring is reflected in policy preferences, and as a consequence there is substantial agreement within, and substantial disagreement between, various Italian political parties on important public issues. We will now add elite opinions to our analysis and show that policy differences are increasingly party related at the elite level, with elites of a particular party being in substantial agreement on most issues.

It is obvious that Italian politics does not revolve solely around a single, neatly ordered dimension. Historically, many dimensions have been important in Italian politics. Most of them are still current in debate: They vary in importance, but few disappear and fewer are resolved. The existence of a number of parties is itself evidence of dimensions, for though several parties could exist based on different cutting points of a single dimension, it is highly unlikely. Hence we must reconcile the existence of multiple dimensions with the predictive power of the single left-right measure.

We can simplify the problem at the outset by pointing out that the dimensions responsible for the existence of minor parties seem to attract the attention of few voters. For example, the parties of the left are anticlerical; the DC is proclerical; the right is in part less clerical than the DC, but it attracts relatively few votes and hence attenuates only slightly the strong association between left and right and sympathy for the clergy. Similar dynamics hold for foreign policy, in which, for example, the MON and MSI are less pro-American than the parties to the immediate left of them. Thus it is possible for strong relationships to emerge even when the parties of the right revert toward the attitudes of the left on many variables. Taking this phenomenon into account, it is important that our two largest groups, the left and center, represent opposite positions on most dimensions. The problem of conflicting dimensions is minimal, since they are largely reinforcing, at least in this election and for most voters.

At this point we will introduce our measures of policy dimensions. We began by identifying those dimensions that have been most salient in Italian politics. These turned out to fall along socioeconomic, religious (or clerical-anticlerical), foreign policy, and traditional-modern dimensions. We then experimented with questions that seemed to tap these dimensions and finally decided on the following questions, listed with the short title used to identify them henceforth in the chapter.

In the division of the national income workers are really in an unfavorable position (workers disfavored).

Italian foreign policy ought to be entirely independent of the United States (independent foreign policy).

We ought to stop financing Church schools and spend more money on state schools (church education).

It's sad to see the traditions and good breeding of earlier times disappear in Italy (traditions disappear).

We ought to have a law in Italy permitting divorce (divorce law).

Young people ought to receive the greatest amount of education possible even if it means sacrifices for their families (more education).

Capitalism represents a danger for Italy (capitalism a danger).

Labor unions have too much power in Italy (unions too powerful).

The distribution of responses by party is shown in table 26. It is clear from the table that some items expected to differentiate among the parties do not do so. Some things are supported by everyone, at least in principle, and consequently are not divisive. These "valence" issues will be discussed later.

TABLE 26
Agreement on Issues by Party
(Mass Sample)

ISSUE	STRONGLY AGREE OR AGREE (%)							
	PCI	PSIUP	PSI-PSDI	PRI	DC	PLI	MON	MSI
Workers disfavored	96	87	85	93	80	55	83	78
Ind. foreign policy	93	91	68	62	42	38	44	41
Church education	92	87	76	77	47	56	33	57
Traditions disappear	81	73	74	85	86	85	86	92
Divorce law	64	61	52	50	19	44	42	37
More education	85	96	91	93	94	84	93	89
Capitalism a danger	91	84	63	50	48	21	58	49
Unions too powerful	36	21	31	50	51	63	80	73

The other items are "position" issues on which the parties do differ in important ways. In the light of the previous discussion of left-right differences, it is important that the line of division between left and right seems to be drawn differently according to the issue. Parties are not consistently left or right across the entire spectrum of issues. How-

107

ever, in most cases the distributions of opinions are transitive, that is, there is very little turning back to a more leftist position as one moves from the center parties to the right. When this does occur the differences are not great and the numbers of people involved are small. An example is that supporters of the three rightist parties are more in favor of an independent foreign policy than the supporters of the Christian Democratic party.

But the division between left and right is drawn at different points on the party spectrum for different issues. Thus socioeconomic questions, such as workers disfavored, find the Socialists and Republicans on the left, while other questions tapping the same dimension, such as capitalism a danger and unions too powerful, find the Socialists and Republican mass publics siding with the center and right. It is of particular importance that the elites of the Socialist party (the Republican elites were not investigated) give a pattern of responses that reflects their ideological position. On the foreign policy dimension, on the other hand, the leftist position is shared only by the Communists and their Social Proletarian allies. The DC position on religious questions is shared only with Monarchists, who seem to be even more Catholic than the DC supporters on the Catholic schools question. The question of divorce gave rise to an interesting pattern of responses (remember that this was 1968). The mass publics of all the parties were rather divided; differences were not very great except for the strong opposition to divorce of the Christian Democrats. Yet, at the elite level the Communists and Socialists were strongly and overwhelmingly supportive of the right to divorce.

On all of these questions the most clearcut differences are between Communists and Christian Democrats. As these parties have the largest electorates, it is clear why there is such a strong overall relationship between party and policy preference: The parties that do not fit are small and do not count for much statistically, though their political clout and sensitive location may give them considerable political importance.

There is greater coherence between policy preference and party choice on the part of elites than masses. There is considerable evidence from other studies that the relationship between policy and ideology is much stronger for party elites than for the rank and file. McCloskey has reported this for the United States. [9] Barnes has shown this for a sample of Italian Socialists. [10] Perhaps it is ideology that leads to coherence between policy preferences and party choice. Whatever is the reason, the greater coherence exists in Italy.

We have identified a number of the items that best predict party differences and combined them in a left-right policy scale. They were selected through a factor analysis of agreement items that yielded a varimax rotated factor matrix with three factors. The first factor, and the one utilized here, had four items that loaded heavily: workers disfavored, independent foreign policy, church education, and capitalism a danger. The second factor combined two items in a traditionalism factor, and the third was based on the two religious items. We have coded all respondents on the four item left-right policy scale. The availability of "agree strongly," "agree," "disagree," and "disagree strongly" permitted a more refined coding system; we have taken advantage of this, stretching the respondents out along a much more extensive dimension and then picking cutting points that divided the mass sample into four groups of roughly equal size. The importance of closeness to party for insuring a good fit between policy position and partisan identification is demonstrated by table 27. There is no reason

TABLE 27
Left-Right Policy Scale and Partisan Identification by Closeness to Party

	GAMMA
Party member	.75
Very close	.63
More or less close	.52
Not very close	.41
DK, no answer	.33

NOTE.—The left-right policy scale is constructed from the loadings of four items on a left-right policy factor; partisan identification is the left-right listing of the parties.

to belabor this point further. There is a close relationship between policy preference and partisan identification, and this relationship is stronger among those with closer attachment to party. It is strongest of all among members of the party and weakest among those who claim identification with the party but are unable to articulate the strength of their identification with it.

But left-right self-placement is still a better predictor of party identification than is any single issue or combination of issues. This is demonstrated by a stepwise multiple regression analysis. In order to meet better the assumptions of interval data the 0–100 self-placement of respondents on scales of sympathy toward clerics, unions, and Americans was used instead of the ordinal level responses to the policy questions. With party identification the dependent variable, left-right placement alone accounts for 42.8 percent of the total variance. Attitudes toward clerics add an additional 5.7 percent; attitudes toward unions explain an additional 2.9 percent beyond that; attitudes toward Americans add a final 1.2 percent, for a total variance explained of 52.6 percent.

Ordered dimensions, it will be recalled, refer to the characteristic of a dimension that parties may be assigned different positions on it. "Position" issues can be so ranked, while "valence" issues cannot. We can divide our set of issues into these two categories and look at their relationship to partisan identification. Our procedure is to determine which are the issues that people say are important to them and then investigate which are the ones that in fact are highly associated with partisan identification. We assume that the really important issues in determining the respondent's identification are the ones that he associates with his party. Thus we asked whether certain things were important to the respondent and later asked which party struggled the most to achieve these things.

Three issues turned out to be important for everyone: the economic development of Italy, the development of education, and governmental stability. These are typical valence issues, things that are generally favored, with most people seeing their own party as the one that struggles the most to achieve them. But it is obvious from an examination of the strength of the relationship between party identification and perception of which party struggles the most for the issue that these issues do not differentiate among the parties. Table 28 demonstrates this. The position issues, on the other hand, show a diminishing relationship between partisan identification and perception as the issue recedes in importance, as we would expect if the issue is an important one in party choice. In other words, the relationship between partisan identification and perception is strongest for respondents for whom the issue is most important. It is clear that the position issues are the ones that differentiate among the parties. Thus we feel justified in acknowledging that valence issues exist in Italian politics while insisting that they are not very important in determinining how people vote. They are ephemera, halos surrounding a party chosen on other grounds. We may conclude that it is the ordered dimensions that count in Italian politics.

Additional evidence of the fit between ordered dimensions and party is found in the strong relationship between score on the left-right policy scale and party identification. The policy scale is that described above. The overall relationship between scale scores and partisan iden-

TABLE 28

Partisan Identification and "Which Party Struggles the Most to . . ." by Importance of Issue

| | VALENCE ISSUES | | | POSITION ISSUES | | |
	Government Stability	Development of Education	Economic Development	Divorce	Just Division of Income	Independence of U.S.
Very important	.70 (917)	.72 (929)	.75 (1195)	.38 (209)	.64 (821)	.43 (331)
Somewhat important	.75 (285)	.73 (265)	.85 (167)	.22 (198)	.53 (307)	.28 (181)
Not very important	.78 (55)	.61 (24)	.82 (3)	.11 (206)	.18 (65)	.12 (188)
Not at all important	.80 (19)	.80 (4)	–(1)	–.06 (527)	.31 (26)	.01 (193)

NOTE: Measure is tau beta; N respondents is in parentheses.

tificaton is strong; Gamma is .55. Table 29 shows the breakdown by party. The poor fit on the right is apparent, as is presence of large numbers of Christian Democrats without strongly voiced opinions.

TABLE 29
Party Identification and Policy Position
(Percentage of Each Party's Identifiers Taking
Left-to Right Positions)

POLICY POSITION	PCI	PSIUP	PSI-PSDI	PRI	DC	PLI	MON	MSI	No ID	Total
Extreme left 1	67	54	30	21	11	16	7	26	19	24
Moderate left 2	20	32	32	52	23	14	43	21	27	26
Moderate right 3	3	6	14	10	19	18	22	19	15	15
Extreme right 4	1	2	9	10	19	47	14	28	11	14
No response	9	6	15	7	28	5	14	6	28	21
Total %	100	100	100	100	100	100	100	100	100	100
N	279	50	369	29	1,048	56	14	47	517	

We also examined the relationship between partisan identification and each individual issue for elite and mass. The relationship is specially strong for the elite on position issues (see table 30).

TABLE 30
Policy Position and Partisan Identification
(Measure Is Gamma)

Three-party ID X	Mass	Councilor	Deputy
Workers disfavored	.42	.80	.50
Church education	.59	.87	1.00
Traditions disappear	.12	.39	.39
Divorce law	.58	.91	.92
More education	−.08	.24	−.07
Capitalism a danger	.51	.81	.26
Labor unions too powerful	.27	.41	.56

The assumption of common elite-mass preferences on political issues is the easiest of all to demonstrate for Italy—up to a point. The structure of political conflict ensures that only the most poorly informed are unaware of the orientations of the politicians and parties on the major issues. But there are many poorly informed members of the electorate.[11] Moreover, within some parties there are internal issue differences that affect the fit between issue position and partisan identification. The Socialists, for example, include respondents who undoubtedly at other times supported the separate PSI and PSDI; these differed on some issues. Finally, the elite measures are based on members of only the three largest parties, which are the ones that best fit the model.

The relationship between elite and mass perceptions can be summarized as follows: The elite are like the mass, only more so. The elite hold in an exaggerated form the opinions of the mass. Or perhaps the mass hold in attenuated form the opinions of the elite. For the relationship between opinion and party is much stronger within the elite than the mass, and strikingly so on the dimensions that have been demonstrated to be extremely important for determining behavior—the clerical and socioeconomic areas. Unfortunately, we unwisely omitted the question dealing with foreign policy from the communal elite interview schedule, so elite and mass cannot be compared on that dimension.

This analysis has pointed out the overall similarities between elite and mass. An additional aspect of the relationship that merits special attention is the "extremism" of the Christian Democratic mass on a number of issues. We use the word "extremism" in a special sense: We find that, contrary to usual expectations, the Christian Democratic mass exhibits more extreme views than the DC elite. It is a common phenomenon in scientific measurement that extreme measures tend to regress toward the mean on remeasurement or in larger populations. But on several sensitive issues of Italian politics we find that the DC communal elite is closer than the DC mass to the all-party mean.

This finding is based on scores for the mass and communal councilors on the degree of sympathy felt for various groups and countries on a 0–100 scale, with 50 representing neutral affect. The scores of the two groups are close together, and in almost every case the mass scores are closer to the national means, that is, were less extreme, than the scores of the councilors. However, in six out of the total of forty-five cases (fifteen objects of sympathy and three parties), mass opinions were further than the opinions of councilors from the all-party mass mean, and all six of these involved Christian Democrats. As table 31 demonstrates, the DC mass identifiers are more proclerical (73 to 61) than the councilors, more pro-American (61 to 57), more sympathetic to big business (47 to 43), less sympathetic to Russians (20 to 24), less sympathetic to the PSI/PSDI (46 to 52), and less sympathetic to unions (60 to 64).

This suggests that DC elites work under considerable constraints in

113

TABLE 31
Elite-Mass Scores
(Sympathy for . . .)

	PCI		PSI-PSDI		DC		NATIONAL MEAN
	Councilor	Mass	Councilor	Mass	Councilor	Mass	Mass
Unions	87	79	77	70	64	60	65
Clergy	14	31	30	48	61	73	58
Small business	60	56	61	54	60	53	54
Big business	7	19	25	35	43	47	38
Americans	8	25	36	46	57	61	51
Germans	18	25	25	28	34	30	30
Russians	75	66	29	34	24	20	32
English	28	32	42	40	40	39	38
French	45	41	29	36	31	35	37
Chinese	51	45	17	24	11	17	24
PCI	94	87	27	38	11	17	35
DC	16	26	43	52	90	86	64
PSI-PSDI	30	41	93	77	52	46	50
PSIUP	75	62	18	32	12	21	32
Center-left	18	37	82	68	75	58	54

the opening to the left and that they are in fact ahead of their electorate in moving toward the national mean. Note, however, that the spread between elite and mass is small; it is only the direction of the difference, not its magnitude, that merits attention. In most cases the gap between elite and mass is much greater for the PCI and PSI/PSDI, but in these parties the mass is nearer the national mean. It is in fact probably the extremism of the elites of the two leftist parties that accounts for the consistent regression of their mass identifiers toward the national mean. In the case of the DC, however, the errant choices of the mass cannot be explained away. Though small, the differences on general affect questions do seem to have important consequences. But, as we have seen, they are not translated into differences between elite and mass in policy preferences.

From the foregoing it is clear that spatial models of politics correspond nicely with the reality world of the Italian electorate as it has been operationalized in this study. This finding has implications for a wide range of considerations. Probably the most important is that it demonstrates that multiple dimensions of political conflict originating in diverse ages and circumstances need not be overlapping. Italian political conflict reflects many issue dimensions that are not historically necessarily connected, though we have shown them to be in fact closely related. As new issues have arisen they have tended to be superimposed along the lines of old cleavages rather than crisscrossing them.

This is not to claim that cross-cutting cleavages do not exist. The difficulties between the center and right illustrate the dynamics of political conflict in Italy. The Liberals were traditionally an anticlerical party, and they are still less clerical than the Christian Democrats. But because of the challenge of the left, as well as other reasons, this issue is played down today and the anticlerical aspect of liberalism has lost its political saliency. Another example is nationalism: The MSI is quite nationalistic, but the importance of other conflicts in Italian politics keeps the party from being as anti-American as the leftist parties. In a similar way, issues originating in the counterreformation, the industrial revolution, and the cold war are transformed into poles of a single left-right dimension.

If the issue dimensions of Italian politics were as clear-cut as suggested above, there would be little reason for the multiparty system. Yet it is clear that voter opinions support such a system and, indeed, perhaps require it. For it is the mass parties that fit the left-right space best, and it is the size of their electorates that makes the relationships so strong. Due to their size they are able in large part to define the issues and to impose their definitions on the electorate, and these are the issues that we have studied. While we cannot predict with confidence the future of these issues, their anchorage in the mass parties and the slow pace of change in the Italian system suggest that they may be around for quite a while.

8

Representatives and the Represented

Representation in Italy has been conceptualized in this study as the representation of institutionalized traditions. While the party is the principal organizational mobilizer for the tradition, it is still only one component of a complex mix of institutions, ideologies, interests, subcultures, and family legacies that make up the traditions. Previous chapters have examined these components of the traditions and have thus indirectly revealed many aspects of the relationships between representatives and the represented. In this chapter we now look directly at the relations between the individuals involved—the representatives and the represented.

VARIETIES OF LINKAGES

Representation involves the linking of elites and mass publics. Linkages can take many forms, and none of them can claim universal acceptance as the most significant variety. The nature of the "right" form of linkage is a philosophical and normative question; that is the assumption that has guided our conceptualization of representation. Moreover, competing dimensions of representation can exist within the same political system. This is certainly the case in Italy, and in this chapter we will examine several of these dimensions before looking at linkages in issues, which has been the most widely utilized operationalization of linkage in studies of representation.

Isomorphism in social background is widely regarded as an important form of representative linkage; dozens of social background studies attest to its appeal and cross-national utility. We have already shown that the elites of all Italian parties, at both the local and national levels, are quite atypical of their electorates. Only the PCI has a substantial working-class representation, and even that party is led by well-educated personnel of largely middle-class background. Whether desirable or not, social isomorphism is of little importance in the process of representation in Italy.

Perhaps this absence of social isomorphism is not surprising, since the religious dimension is as important as the class dimension in Italian politics. And as we have already shown, religious behavior differs greatly between the parties: All but one of the Christian Democratic deputies claim to attend church weekly, while none of the Communists and only one of the Socialists make this claim. Furthermore, most of the PCI and PSI/PSDI elites, and virtually all of the deputies of those parties, claim to be atheists or agnostics on matters of religion, even if few of their voters make this claim. So on this very important dimension elite behavior fits the expectations of the traditions; if one considers religious practice to be the most important line of cleavage, it is possible to conclude that there is substantial isomorphism along the basic cleavage dimension of the Italian polity.

Much of the debate over representation has focused on the relationship between representatives and the represented in the realm of beliefs, class interests, and issues. This classic debate has dominated American research on representation and certainly reflects a very important variety of linkage. Our previous chapters have demonstrated the considerable measure of agreement that exists between the two parts of the dyad on the ideological or general belief systems level and on left-right placement of the self and the parties. Moreover, we have shown that the broad appeal of the larger Italian parties makes it difficult to relate parties to specific class interests, though it is clear that the basic tendencies of each party are closer to the interests of one group than another.

This previous concern with beliefs and class interests leaves issues to be considered here. One method of measuring this relationship or linkage is to examine the impact that variations in the views of the represented have on the views of the representatives, or at least to examine their covariation, since causation is not easily demonstrated. This can be accomplished through the analysis of the opinions of both on issues, through the relating of mass opinion to the legislative behavior of the representative, or through both methods.

We decided against the analysis of roll-call votes in Italy on the

117

grounds that the potential payoff did not merit the investment. Voting in the Chamber of Deputies is by roll call on many issues, in which case almost all deputies accept party discipline. But voting is secret when a substantial minority requests it. As a consequence, most of the important and controversial votes are secret. Members sometimes vote against their parties on these ballots, but individual deviations cannot be documented. However, we are able to examine the linkage through the use of attitude measures and through the statements of elites and masses concerning what are the most important questions facing the country. The exploration of these linkages is a major focus of this chapter.

Another form of linkage is direct: the personal ties that exist between deputies and their constituents. We will examine the extent to which respondents claim personal acquaintance with a representative and the nature of the face-to-face relationships that the deputies maintain with their constituents.

The final aspect of linkage that we will consider is the normative evaluation of the process. What do constituents in Italy expect from their representatives? What are the expectations of the latter? Is there conflict between their mutual expectations?

We will conclude the chapter with an examination of how parties, representatives, and unions and professional organizations are rated by the mass respondents as defenders of their interests. This will enable us to place the parties in perspective with other components of the traditions.

ISSUES AS LINKAGE

Briefly stated, the argument concerning the nature of the agreement between deputies and their constituencies assumes that in a truly representative system the level of agreement will be high: Representatives should reflect the views of their constituents on the salient issues of the day.

What these issues are, of course, is itself a problem. A great deal of political debate is over what the agenda of politics should be, and that aspect is often as important as partisan position on particular issues. Our analysis of issues will be based on the questions introduced earlier in the study, which were formulated to tap the dimensions that seemed to dominate Italian politics. These questions sharply differentiate among the parties and thus meet our purposes. Moreover, other evidence presented in this study has shown that the questions also tap several fundamental issue areas of Italian politics. The questions are those presented in the previous chapter.

Throughout this study we have emphasized the importance of the party as a mediator between representatives and their constituents. Since parties are so salient and the issues chosen reflect those on which the parties differ, it is not surprising that there are substantial party-related differences in attitudes toward issues. But the level of agreement within the parties—especially on the left—and the disagreement among the parties is very striking, and especially so on what we have previously identified as "position" rather than "valence" issues.

This is particularly true at the elite level. As table 32 demonstrates, there is virtual unanimity among Communist deputies on almost all of the issues. And on most of these issues this agreement is shared with the councilmen and the mass publics. The question on which there is least agreement concerns traditions. This is hardly political—or rather it is hardly seen as political by the mass publics and, perhaps, the councilmen. On the other hand, PCI deputies, with their greater sophistication, gave answers congruent with their self image as modernizers.

TABLE 32

Issue Agreement between Elite and Mass

(% Who Agree or Strongly Agree)

ISSUE	PCI			PSI-PSDI			DC		
	Mass	Coun-cilor	Deputy	Mass	Coun-cilor	Deputy	Mass	Coun-cilor	Deputy
Workers dis-favored	96	98	100	85	91	86	80	71	66
Independent foreign pol-icy	93	*	100	68	*	64	42	*	43
Church education	92	96	100	76	98	100	47	34	20
Traditions dis-appear	81	47	14	74	60	52	86	77	69
Divorce law	64	98	100	52	98	97	19	18	11
More educa-cation	85	80	69	91	87	100	94	94	98
Capitalism a danger	91	99	100	63	80	48	48	37	30
Unions too powerful	36	14	7	31	36	0	51	42	19

*Question not asked.

Answers on the divorce question reflect the lack of enthusiasm of PCI sympathizers with the divorce movement, at least in 1968. By the time of the 1974 referendum, opinions had evolved considerably.[1] Yet the level of PCI elite agreement is striking. On the other hand, that 36 percent of the PCI identifiers consider unions too powerful is difficult to understand. We have no explanation for this finding, other than to point to the absence of sharp differences among all three mass publics on this question.

The consensus among PSI-PSDI supporters and elites is considerable, but not as high as within the PCI. This is perhaps fitting in a party torn between reform and revolution, at least on the ideological level. On heavily ideological subjects, such as divorce, church schools, and education, there is almost complete agreement among PSI-PSDI deputies and only slightly less among councilmen. Socialist mass publics, on the other hand, reflect greater disagreement than the PCI mass.

The DC possesses the largest amount of disagreement, as befits a party that attempts to reconcile diverse points of view. In all cases we find the DC councilmen's scores between those of the deputies and mass, seemingly indicating that they are closer than the deputies to the opinions of the DC rank and file.

Our next task is to see whether the differences that we have just observed among the elite are due to differences in the constituencies. If we take territory as the unit that is represented, as in the United States or the United Kingdom, then the views of the representatives should be related to the views of the represented in the constituency; that is, there should be a strong correlation between the views of elites and their constituents.

First, we must describe how we obtained these measures of association. Italian constituencies are large, with as many as forty-seven representatives being elected in a single constituency in 1968. Deputies seldom feel that they represent a subsection of the constituency; indeed, they indicate the nation as a whole as their point of reference.[2] Thus, while it would be possible in many—and probably most—cases to relate a deputy to a province or smaller area in which he is known to have close political ties, there are no theoretical reasons for doing so. Moreover, the large constituency gives us means for each party based on a sufficient number of cases to give us increased confidence in our interpretation of the results.

Using the constituencies for the Chamber of Deputies as the representative units creates some conceptual problems in assessing issue linkages between mass publics and communal councilmen. However, the councilmen were selected from a sample of one-fourth of the sampling units (communes) of the mass sample, hence we would have to discard three-fourths of the mass sample if we were to look only at the relationships within the communes. Perhaps that would be acceptable if the number interviewed in each commune were larger, but by the time the sample within the commune is divided by party preference the number is too small to be meaningful. Consequently, we are examining the relationship between the views of the individual communal councilor and the mean score on the same issue of all of the identifiers with his party in the constituency from which deputies are elected. Obviously we are unable to tap differences that reflect idiosyncratic aspects of local politics. On the other hand, we are looking at issues that are essentially national and on which great local—as opposed to regional—differences are hardly to be expected. If the principal differences in opinion in Italy are sectional, we would expect them to be revealed by the use of this level of aggregation. If, on the other hand, they stem from essentially local concerns, this method would not uncover them.

There were thirty-two multimember constituencies in Italy in 1968, and twenty-eight of these were represented in our sample of deputies. They contained 2,296 of our mass respondents, ranging from a minimum of thirteen to a maximum of 207 per constituency, with eighty-two being the mean number. Consequently, even when divided—inevitably unevenly—among the three parties, there is a reasonably large number on which to base the means.

Our results show that there are no strong relationships between representatives' opinions and those of their party's identifiers living in the constituencies. Table 33 demonstrates this quite well. In most cases the association is weak or nonexistent because there is no variance to be explained. The .58 correlation between Communist deputies and supporters on "Capitalism a danger" is a statistical artifact; examination of the scatterplot shows two cases inexplicably so deviant that the computation yielded this r. Constituency simply explains very little of the variation within the parties.

However, if we look at the representativeness of the system itself rather than simply the relationships *within* the parties, the correlations between elite and mass are much stronger. Table 34 demonstrates the importance that party differences make in strengthening the correlation coefficients. Thus, the "constituency" column (A) presents the relationship between each deputy and the mean of *all the respondents* in his electoral constituency. The "party identifiers" column (B) shows

TABLE 33

Issue Agreement between Elite and Mass

(Measure is r between Elite Opinion and Party Identifiers
in the Electoral Constituency for the Chamber of Deputies)

	PCI		PSI-PSDI		DC	
ISSUE	Deputy	Coun-cilor	Deputy	Coun-cilor	Deputy	Coun-cilor
Workers disfavored	.00	−.08	.01	.25	.20	.09
Independent foreign policy	.00	*	.00	*	.28	*
Church education	.00	−.11	.00	−.03	.16	−.02
Traditions disappear	.13	.06	−.23	.20	.16	−.04
Divorce law	.12	−.10	.26	.08	−.05	−.03
More education	−.03	−.02	.00	.39	.02	.11
Capitalism a danger	.58	−.09	.01	.33	−.22	−.04
Unions too powerful	−.33	.27	−.15	−.05	.11	.09

*Question not posed.

the correlation between each deputy and the mean for *the supporters of his party* in the constituency, lumping all of the parties together. It is apparent that the mean opinion of all of the respondents in the constituency explains very little. Party, on the other hand, raises the strength of the relationships tremendously, especially on what we have previously labeled "position," rather than "valence," issues.

Representation, it has been argued, is the normative dimension of mobilization; as a normative problem, it is not possible to specify what

TABLE 34

Systemic Representation
Issue Agreement between Elite and Mass
(Measure is r in Electoral Constituency for Chamber of Deputies)

	A. ELITE OPINION AND MEAN MASS OPINION IN CONSTITUENCY		B. ELITE OPINION AND MEAN MASS OPINION OF PARTY IDENTIFIERS	
ISSUE	Deputy	Councilor	Deputy	Councilor
Workers disfavored	.11	.09	.33	.31
Independent foreign policy	.00	*	.59	*
Church education	.12	.01	.64	.49
Traditions disappear	.01	.12	.10	.11
Divorce law	.12	.07	.68	.58
More education	.02	.18	.07	.21
Capitalism a danger	−.09	.06	.42	.46
Unions too powerful	.06	.24	.11	.19

*Question not posed.

is "good" or "bad" representation; this varies from system to system depending upon their public philosophies. But if we value similarities in the opinions of representatives and represented, and if we look at the systemic level rather than the individual constituencies, the Italian system exhibits impressively strong relationships between the opinions of elites and masses. Moreover, it is party differences, rather than constituency differences, that are important. Once again the central role of the party is confirmed.

We have demonstrated that there is substantial agreement on most issues within the parties and substantial disagreement between them on most issues of Italian politics. Similar patterns emerge when we examine views of the importance of these same issues (see table 35). We asked the councilors and mass publics how important they considered four of the issues to be, and table 35 presents the percentage at each level for whom the issue was "very important." Economic development is important for everyone in all of the parties. So is a just distribution of income with the inexplicable exception of the DC mass publics. Governmental stability is considerably more important for the governing parties than for the opposition Communists; moreover, within the former it is more important to the elite than the mass, while within the latter it is the reverse. The divorce law emerges as the most party related of all, with the leftist elites attaching far more importance to it in 1968 than did the leftist mass publics. Taken together these findings underline the importance of party in structuring opinion—or at least in reflecting opinions given structure by other means.

TABLE 35
Importance of Issue
(% Who Found These Issues Very Important)

	PCI		PSI-PSDI		DC	
	Councilor	Mass	Councilor	Mass	Councilor	Mass
Governmental stability	42	58	81	73	89	71
Divorce law	61	24	59	23	8	9
Just distribution of income	95	80	93	72	79	57
Economic development	95	88	97	91	95	84

Our final example of issues as linkages deas with perceptions of the most important problems facing Italy. Here the most striking finding is the similarities in the perceptions of the mass publics of the three parties. The largest difference involves 10 percent more PCI than DC identifiers listing housing as an important problem (see table 36). Al-

TABLE 36
Most Important Problems Facing Italy
(% of Deputy, Councilor, and Mass Samples Mentioning)

	PCI			PSI-PSDI			DC		
	Deputy	Coun-cilor	Mass	Deputy	Coun-cilor	Mass	Deputy	Coun-cilor	Mass
General prob-lems	0	17	2	14	22	2	9	23	4
Political insti-tutions and practices	27	3	13	36	12	22	44	9	19
Income	11	19	33	14	12	30	7	13	31
Housing and work	15	0	29	14	2	20	12	1	19
Other per-sonal eco-nomic prob-lems	8	9	7	0	22	6	0	21	6
National eco-nomic prob-lems	11	43	5	7	5	5	2	6	4
Foreign Af-fairs—war and peace	23	6	4	0	17	3	2	18	4
Miscella-neous, in-cluding prob-lems of young	4	4	7	14	6	12	23	5	13

though greater, the differences at the elite level are modest compared with those we described in dealing with issues. In general, deputies emphasize political institutions and practices. The 43 percent of Communist councilmen coded under national economic problems were almost all concerned with the injustices of national tax policy. The most striking difference is the PCI deputies' seeming monopoly of concern with foreign affairs and especially questions of war and peace. On the other hand, DC and PSI- PSDI deputies are impressively ahead of the PCI in the expression of concern for the problems of the young.

The pattern just described suggests that the differences between the parties, especially at the mass level, may not be as great as they appear to be. That is, when the subject is a set of issues chosen because it included the major dimensions of disagreement among parties, great differences emerge. But when mass publics spontaneously recall what they consider to be most important—and not necessarily what separates the parties—there is substantial agreement. Of course, they may favor different solutions for the problems. Nevertheless, it seems possible that much of the public debate in Italy that focuses on the "big issues" masks a great deal of consensus at the mass level on what the "real issues" should be. But one thing is well established by our data: The big differences derive from party and are not related to differences among the constituencies.

CONTACTS AS LINKAGE

Regardless of the variety of representation involved, some kind of contact between representative and represented seems to be ubiquitous. Of course, the nature varies from system to system. The representative may be a remote figure whose ties are mediated through organizations and other brokerage relationships, or he may be personally known to those he represents. But contacts of some kind are a major form of linkage.

In a clientelistic polity personal contacts would be the most important form of linkage; indeed, they could be the only form. We are convinced that clientelism plays a very important role in Italian politics—in all parties, but especially within the right parties. However, while it is easy to theorize about clientelism, it is difficult to operationalize it for investigation in a nation-wide survey. Clientelism lends itself more readily to intensive investigation of particular communities or sociometric studies of interactions. It is problematical whether questions can be formulated for a mass sample that would effectively capture clientelistic orientations. We have not attempted to do so. As a result, we must rely on indirect measures, and these will accomplish little more than to show the highly personalistic nature of the political process within Italian parties. Moreover, while clientelism is of considerable importance in Italian electoral politics, it is in the policy process, the "policy game" as opposed to the "electoral game," that it is most important. And this study has concentrated on the electoral game.

The data reveal the substantial differences that exist between the parties of left, center, and right. Although limited, these data serve to place in perspective the heretofore predominant role of party organization in our analysis. In all parties, personalistic contacts are impressive, yet it is difficult to relate these to larger concerns. They involve personal favors, advice, and so on. We are reminded of the finding of Verba and Nie that particularized contacts do not seem related to collective goals and hence are different in their consequences from other forms of participation.[3] This kind of linkage can coexist with strong party organizations and need not have any impact on substantive political issues. We will indicate that there are extensive contacts between representatives and their constituents, especially in the right parties. However, a more extensive analysis of patron-client relationships lies outside the scope of this study.

We find that a very large percentage of the respondents claims a personal acquaintanceship with a deputy or senator. Without data from other countries it is impossible to evaluate these results in comparative perspective. Table 37 shows the portion claiming a personal acquaintanceship, as well as the portion that claims to have written to a senator or deputy. The common pattern of the PRI and the three parties of the

TABLE 37

Contacts with Deputies or Senators, by Party

	PCI	PSIUP	PSI-PSDI	PRI	DC	PLI	MON	MSI
Claimed personal acquaintance with senator or deputy (%)	28	20	32	59	28	54	57	54
Had ever written to a senator or deputy (%)	5	6	8	14	8	18	36	17

right stands out, as does the comparatively low ranking of the DC. In fact, that party and the left are similar, and the similarity is especially evident when the results are examined by level of involvement (see table 38). A previous chapter has demonstrated that the Nonvoter category contains many different kinds of people, only some of whom fit the usual pattern of Nonvoters. On all the other categories, except for Party Members, there is an amazing similarity between the left and the DC. Results are similar when educational level is examined by left-DC-right political orientation. The DC identifiers are similar to

TABLE 38

Personal Acquaintanceship with Deputy or Senator, by Level of Involvement and Political Orientation

POLITICAL ORIENTATION	INVOLVEMENT (%)				
	Nonvoter	Vote Only	Passive Participation	Active Participation	Member
Left	22	11	26	47	62
DC	31	14	25	47	71
Right	25	25	52	64	77

those of the left parties, and dissimilar to those of the right parties, in the low and middle educational categories and more similar to the left than the right even in the higher education category (see table 39).

TABLE 39

Personal Acquaintanceship with Deputy or Senator, by Education and Political Orientation

POLITICAL ORIENTATION	EDUCATION (%)		
	Low	Middle	High
Left	26	43	59
DC	23	40	66
Right	33	67	79

These results can be interpreted in diverse ways, so it is unwise to make much out of these findings. But the general tendency to lump the DC with the right when commenting on personalistic elements in Italian politics seems questionable. It is possible that social class rather than mobilization styles account for the similarities. However, the Monarchists are overwhelmingly working class, and so are most of the Neofascist identifiers. Sheer size of party may be the best explanation of all for the level of acquaintanceship, for the largest—the DC and PCI—are similar, while the others trail more or less in order of descending size. Only the PSIUP deviated widely from this pattern, and in 1968 it was a new party with few leaders possessing wide public exposure.

The practice of writing letters to deputies or senators is much more widespread on the right (and PRI) than left or DC (see table 37). The Monarchists are the most prolific in this field, as would be expected from a clientelistic party.

But it is in the receipt of letters that the parties differ most, and closeness to power seems the best explanation (table not shown). For, while no PCI deputy claimed to receive more than 100 letters per week from his constituents, 40 percent of PSI-PSDI deputies and 67 percent of DC deputies made this claim, and 16 percent of the DC deputies claimed to receive more than 500 letters per week from constituents.

While the frequencies associated with each category vary from party to party, there are no dramatic differences in the subject matter of the letters. Most of them concerned personal favors, such as requests for jobs, recommendations, pensions, housing, and the like, as well as intervention with the bureaucracy.

A final form of contacts involves the ties of the deputies with their constituencies. These ties can be sketched out only in very broad strokes, for the small number of deputies in each party and the differences between incumbent and newly elected deputies lead to sparsely populated cells. Several different indicators show that incumbent DC deputies claim fewer contacts with their local parties than is the case with deputies of the two left parties. The party is more important for the newly elected. This reaffirms the conclusion that party is more important for the left and, furthermore, that incumbent DC deputies develop independence from the party. The only other clear finding is the PCI claim of extensive contacts with workers, immigrants, the poor, and so on, as 54 percent of PCI deputies—compared with 12 percent of PSI-PSDI and 8 percent of DC deputies—mentioned these groups. There are, of course, good ideological reasons for this claim, but it may also reflect empirical reality quite well. There are no important differences among the parties in contact with other groups.

While no dramatic findings emerge from our discussion of contacts, one very important general conclusion seems warranted: The predominant importance of party in securing election and in constraining policy alternatives has not done away with personalized contacts. These are widespread in all of the parties and especially so on the right. Moreover, the DC is only slightly more personalistic than the PCI, at least as we have measured this phenomenon here. It seems likely that educational and social class differences in the composition of the parties, their size, and their closeness to power explain more of the variance in personalism than do ideology and mobilization styles.

NORMATIVE EVALUATIONS OF REPRESENTATIVE ROLES

In this section we will examine the role perceptions of deputies and mass publics. In previous chapters, as well as in the first two sections of the present chapter, we have concentrated on what the existing patterns really are, or at least what the elites and mass publics say they are. In the present section we examine what the three groups consider to be proper, what they say the patterns should be.

At the elite level, we rely on a number of questions that probe attitudes toward conflicts in obligations arising from differences of opinion among representatives, their parties, and their electorates. In this way we are able to examine how the representatives say they would resolve conflicts and, in the case of incumbents, how they say they have resolved them as well.

It is clear that the party and especially the parliamentary party is the dominant reference point for the deputies, though there are differences among the parties. Party is more important for the Communists than for the other parties, but it ranks first for all, no matter how it is measured. Personal conviction is in second place among PSI-PSDI and DC deputies, ahead of voters, and in the PCI there is little difference in the rankings of these latter two. That is, in case of conflict between the demands of party, voters, and personal opinions and preferences, most deputies choose party, then personal convictions, and voters last.

Some differences among the parties result from variations in posing the question. For example, our summary question was, "In general, do you believe that a deputy ought to vote according to his personal conviction, as his party asks him, or as his electorate would want?" Table 40 presents the results for incumbent and newly elected deputies combined, omitting those with ambiguous answers. Ten PCI, five PSI-PSDI, and six DC deputies would not make clear choices, arguing, in most cases, that there could be no real conflict, that they, their parties, and their voters were almost always in agreement, and so on.

TABLE 40
How Deputy Should Vote
(%)

	PCI	PSI-PSDI	DC
Deputy should:			
Follow personal conviction	6	22	22
Vote as party asks	82	74	66
Vote as his electorate wants	12	4	12
Total %	100	100	100
N	17	23	41

It is clear that in all parties the parliamentary party comes first. We asked the deputies what they would do in case of a conflict between their wishes and those of their parliamentary groups on a parliamentary vote. All of the Communists, incumbent and newly elected, said they would follow their party. Within the DC, 85 percent of the incumbents and 90 percent of the newly elected chose the party, with the remainder saying they would obey if it were not a matter of conscience. Only among the Socialists was there hesitation: of the incumbents, 64 percent said they would obey, 7 percent would obey if it were not a matter of conscience, and 29 percent said they would abstain or publicly dissent; among the newly elected the figures were 50 percent, 40 percent, and 10 percent. It is likely that the recently achieved merger of the PSI and PSDI had left Socialist deputies uncertain as to how far they were willing to commit themselves to following their party.

Similar patterns emerge when the conflict is between the deputy and his local party. Among incumbents only 7 percent of the DC and none of the other parties' deputies would follow their local party's wishes. Among the newly elected, 25 percent of both PCI and DC deputies would follow the local party. Moreover, among the newly elected, 49 percent of the DC, 40 percent of the PSI-PSDI, and 8 percent of PCI deputies would follow their own convictions, especially on matters of conscience. It seems likely that new deputies start their careers with somewhat unrealistic expectations, especially in the PSI-PSDI and DC.

Personal convictions become dominant only when in conflict with the wishes of a majority of voters in the constituency. Newly elected deputies either denied that such a conflict could arise or gave a variety of answers that meant they would follow their own convictions. Among incumbent Communists, none claimed to have been placed in this position; but when asked what they would do if they were, 50 percent said they would follow the wishes of their voters, 30 percent the party, and 20 percent their own opinions. Since they consistently deny the possibility of conflict, these latter preferences seem hypothetical.

Half of the incumbent Socialists had experienced conflict between their personal preferences and those of their voters. In their statements as to what they would do in case of conflict, 18 percent of the Socialists said they would follow the voters, 36 percent would follow the party, and 46 percent their own opinions.

Among Christian Democrats, 30 percent had experienced conflict. The Christian Democrats are similar to the Socialists in their preferences: 10 percent would follow voters, 39 percent the party, and 45 percent their own opinions.

A summary question will place the previous comparisons in perspective. All the deputies were asked what priority they would give to various considerations in their parliamentary voting. Table 41 presents the results. As would be expected, deputies from parties in the coalition give a higher priority to their relationships with the cabinet. The PCI deputies give far greater priority to the party and voters. In fact, the PCI gives higher priorities in general.

We also investigated the perceptions of the communal councilors on these points. They were asked, "In taking a position on a particular problem, what is the order of importance that you give to the following

TABLE 41
Deputies' Priorities in Parliamentary Voting

	PCI	PSI-PSDI	DC
Percent giving absolute priority to:			
Desire to support or oppose cabinet	19	40	43
Position of parliamentary group	81	61	38
Position of party in the constituency	56	4	4
Position of majority of your voters	67	4	6
Your own personal opinion	21	21	15

opinions?" Through inattention, a few interviewers permitted respondents to place more than one source in first place, so percentages add up to slightly more than 100. It is nevertheless clear that party plays less of a role and personal opinion plays more of one at the communal level, and this is true in all the parties. Indeed, personal opinion at least ties for first place in all the parties, and party ranks third among DC and PCI councilors. The party is obviously less important to councilors than to deputies (see table 42).

TABLE 42
Councilors' Priorities in Decision Making
(Percent Ranking Each in First Place)

	PCI	PSI-PSDI	DC
Party	24	31	16
Voters	34	28	28
Personal opinion	37	31	39
Expert opinion	10	12	19
Total %	105	102	102
N	99	102	125

NOTE: Sum of percents is more than 100 because a few respondents gave first place to more than one.

The previous results related to the elites. When we look at mass-level attitudes toward the same issues, we find, not surprisingly, that mass publics have less regard for the party and the deputy and more for the voters. But, while they rank the voter as more important than does the deputy, they still place the party ahead of the deputy's personal opinion in all parties except those on the right.

At the mass level we have data for identifiers of all of the parties, so we are not limited to the three largest. This is very fortunate, because it demonstrates the great difference between the three right parties and the others, including the DC. Table 43 summarizes the results.

TABLE 43
Mass Public's Views of Deputies' Obligations in
Conflict Situations
(%)

	PCI	PSIUP	PSI-PSDI	PRI	DC	PLI	MON	MSI
	Conflict between Deputy's Conviction and Party Decision							
Deputy should:								
Vote with party	65	56	53	70	54	48	21	49
Depends	6	6	6	9	9	10	14	5
Decide for himself	29	37	41	22	37	42	64	46
Total %	100	99	100	101	100	100	99	100
	Conflict between Deputy's Conviction and Wishes of Voters							
Follow voters	79	69	72	78	72	71	71	53
Decide for himself	21	31	28	22	28	29	29	47
Total %	100	100	100	100	100	100	100	100

The mass identifiers in each party consistently give the party a lower priority than do the deputies of the three major parties, which are of course the only ones for which we have elite data. Nevertheless, in all of the center and left parties—and in none of the right parties—there is a majority for following the party. And while there is almost a majority among PLI and MSI identifiers, Monarchists attach little importance to party.

The greater the involvement in politics, the more likely the respondent is to exhibit the behavior preferences characteristic of his or her party. Thus on the left, the percentage that thinks that the deputy should vote as his party prefers rises from 58 percent in the Vote Only category to 71 percent of the Party Members. Within the DC, there are no differences by level of involvement: 56 percent of the Vote Only and 57 percent of the Party Members choose the party. On the right, 19 percent of the Vote Only category thinks that the deputy should decide for himself, compared with 58 percent of the Party Members.

Our most remarkable finding is the similarity in voters' attitudes toward what the deputy should do in case of a conflict between his preferences and those of his voters: He should follow the voters. Between 69 percent (PSIUP) and 79 percent (PCI) say that he should follow voters' wishes. Only MSI identifiers, who divide almost evenly, would grant considerable autonomy to the deputy; and this is perhaps to be expected in a party that is based on the leadership principle and rigid conceptions of authority.

We have uncovered a small conflict between elite and mass in perceptions of legislative roles. While both place the party ahead of the individual deputy, the mass publics are much less supportive of party than are the elites. And the two groups differ dramatically in their evaluations of the priority that should be granted the views of the deputy and of voters, with each thinking that his views should prevail. Our data also demonstrate the personalistic nature of the Monarchists and the importance of the leader in the MSI. Finally, they indicate that the DC identifiers are more similar on these dimensions to the parties of the left than of the right.

WHO DEFENDS INTERESTS OF MASS PUBLICS?

This chapter will close with an examination of mass publics' expectations as to whom they can depend on to defend their interests. This places party in perspective, contrasting it with unions and professional associations, on the one hand, and elected officials, on the other.

The results seem to reinforce our contention that the electoral game and the policy game intersect only marginally. The question was, "To defend the interests of people like yourself, on whom do you count the most?" Respondents were shown a card and asked to choose among (1) labor unions and professional associations, (2) political parties, and (3) elected officials. Comparatively few respondents mention the party at all, and the identifiers from each party except the PCI rank it third. Table 44 gives the results, which show that, despite electoral support for parties, they are not the "first line of defense" for most people. Not unexpectedly, it is the identifiers of the two extreme parties, the PCI and the MSI, who mention parties most often. No MON supporter

TABLE 44
Who Defends Interests by Party
(%)

	PCI	PSIUP	PSI-PSDI	PRI	DC	PLI	MON	MSI
Unions and professional organizations	60	83	64	56	47	37	67	26
Parties	25	7	16	17	17	21	0	23
Elected officials	15	10	20	26	36	42	33	51
Total %	100	100	100	99	100	100	100	100
N	219	41	264	23	635	39	9	35

mentioned the party, which reinforces our contention that party organization counted for little in that party.

Variation in the importance of elected officials reflects our familiar left-right differences. Parties are increasingly personalistic as we move right on the spectrum. Only the Monarchists are inconsistent; and on this dimension, as on others, the DC merits its center position. If only closeness to power were the explanation, the high percentage in governing parties that mentioned elected officials would be understandable. But the MSI doesn't fit this explanation. Perhaps the weakness of the Neofascist unions and professional associations and the intimacy of its organizational structure help to account for its high—the highest of all the parties—reliance on elected officials. But the most likely explanation is related to our initial distinction between the electoral game and the policy game. Party is of paramount importance in the first. In the policy game it is the unions and professional organizations, especially on the left, and elected officials, especially on the center and right, that are most important. This is confirmation of the significance of other components of the institutionalized tradition. The party as an organization plays its greatest role in the electoral game. It is fitting that this chapter should close with our empirical evidence placing the party back in the perspective of the tradition of which it is the chief electoral mobilizer.

9

Representatives and Parties

The organizational importance of the political party has long been recognized in those countries in which it serves as the mediator between representatives and constituents. The previous chapter has demonstrated that this is the case in Italy, where the party is the chief electoral agent in the institutionalization of the political tradition. The party serves as guardian, interpreter, conscience, and mobilizer for the tradition. The nature of the role varies with the party, of course. Clientelism exists in varying degrees in all Italian parties; indeed, it is a feature of politics everywhere. But it is mainly in the parties of the right and, in some areas, the center that traditional patron-client relationships so intrude on the electoral process that the party organization sometimes is effectively bypassed. Indeed, one of the most intriguing aspects of Italian party organization—exemplified by the PCI and, to a lesser extent, the Socialist and Christian Democratic parties—is the way in which modern organizational forms have transformed clientelism, with the party becoming a kind of institutionalized patron, itself performing the protective and mediating function often carried out by patron-politicians.

Because of the importance of party, considerable attention must be devoted to the way in which the party as an organization intrudes on the relationship between representative and represented. Unlike some other countries, the Italian party organization plays the most important role in representation. It controls nominations, coordinates and dominates the campaign, and even after the election continues to intervene in subtle and direct ways in the process.

135

A balanced perspective is necessary. The role of the party remains great even if the impact of the individual representative can be demonstrated. The ability of an individual to influence a role varies, and for representatives party is the most important source of that variation.

This chapter concludes the analysis of the linkage between representative and the represented. Earlier chapters have linked constituents to the parties and the traditions that they present. The previous chapter demonstrated the predominant role of party. The present chapter examines the link between the representative and his party. It concentrates first on political careers and then on the nomination and electoral processes. While it is primarily concerned with describing these two processes, it contributes to our theoretical understanding of representation in Italy through its linking of the representative and the political party as joint agents of the tradition.

POLITICAL CAREERS

The examination of political career patterns has long been an important source of understanding about political systems. It lends itself to quantitative treatment, and a great deal of information can be obtained from official biographies and public sources. Moreover, these sources can be supplemented with questionnaires and interviews. The importance and accessibility of parliamentary elites have resulted in an impressive body of research carried out in a variety of settings and hence a rich source of information about the *cursus honorum* of political man.[1]

It is difficult to evaluate the contribution of this type of research to the generation and validation of propositions with cross-national utility. Searing argues that because patterns differ so much from country to country the compilation of socioeconomic data on the background of elites is a dead end for cross-national comparative purposes.[2] Perhaps this is true. It is not necessary to resolve this question in the present study, for the value of the analysis of career patterns for interparty comparisons within a single country seems obvious. We can point out the substantial differences among parties and the very different roles played by the party organizations in facilitating political careers.

Fortunately, it is possible to relate the findings of this particular study to more general information about Italian deputies. A study of Italian parliamentarians directed by Giovanni Sartori, in collaboration with S. Somogyi, L. Lotti, and A. Predieri, provides an excellent background for evaluating data from the present study.[3] As a word of caution, it should be recalled that Sartori studied all of the deputies who served in postwar legislatures through 1963, while our data refer to a sample of deputies elected in 1968 from the three major parties. We present the Sartori results for these same three major parties; even so, as the Sartori data refer to several different legislatures, conclusions that compare the 1968 (fifth) legislature with previous ones are extremely tentative and hazardous. Although only three parties are represented in our data, they contained 80.5 percent of the members of the Chamber elected in 1968. In terms of the three-party vote, the 1968 deputy sample underrepresents the PCI by 7 percent and overrepresents the PSI-PSDI by 10 percent and the DC by 4 percent. As a result of these sampling procedures, global comparisons with the Sartori findings are impossible. Instead, they will be utilized to highlight important similarities and differences among the parties.

Joining the Party

Sartori and others writing about the Italian party system have emphasized its dominance, at least in the late 1960s, by the generation that reached political maturity at the end of the Second World War. The university-trained segment of this age group formed a highly politicized cohort, and it seems obvious that the more class-conscious elements of the working class also acquired an unusually high degree of commitment to political parties and political solutions. It was an age cohort that came to politics very young in life, formed by its reaction to fascism, the resistance, and the promise of a bright future. These effects are especially apparent on the left, as fully half of the Communist deputies and 42 percent of the Socialists in the sample had joined their parties by age 21. Forty-two percent of the Christian Democrats and only 12 percent of the PCI and 22 percent of the PSI-PSDI deputies in the samples were over thirty years of age when they joined (see table 45).

It is even more surprising that two-thirds of our 1968 deputy sample had joined before 1945, though the interviews date from twenty-three years later. The differences between the two leftist parties show up here as elsewhere, as 93 percent of the PCI and only 43 percent of the PSI-PSDI deputies had joined by that time. Similar patterns exist among the councilors as well (see table 46). This extraordinary domination of the PCI by a cohort with similar formative experiences is important in understanding both the world view of that party's leaders and some of the problems the party faces in modifying its image and increasing its flexibility.

The reasons given for joining the party are quite varied. Ideology is cited most often in all three parties, though it has different connota-

TABLE 45
Age when Joined Party
(%)

AGE	PCI Sartori	PCI 1968 Deputy	PCI 1968 Councilor	PSI-PSDI Sartori	PSI-PSDI 1968 Deputy	PSI-PSDI 1968 Councilor	DC Sartori	DC 1968 Deputy	DC 1968 Councilor
21 or below (Councilor 20 or blw.)	50	41	34	42	39	20	20	25	33
22–30 (Councilor 21–29)	36	56	49	33	29	41	35	51	39
31–40 (Councilor 30–39)	7	4	15	15	29	32	30	19	19
41 + (Councilor 40 +)	5	0	3	7	4	7	12	4	8
Never or missing data	3	0	0	4	0	0	4	0	0
Total %	101	101	101	101	101	100	101	99	99
N	243	27	107	186	28	117	425	47	132

*Computed from Giovanni Sartori et al., *Il parlamento italiano, 1946–1963* (Napoli: Edizioni scientifiche italiane, 1963), p. 87.

TABLE 46
When Joined Party
(%)

DATE	DEPUTIES			COUNCILORS		
	PCI	PSI-PSDI	DC	PCI	PSI-PSDI	DC
Before 1945	93	43	66	50	27	20
1946–49	4	18	17	21	22	23
1950–59	4	36	11	20	24	39
1960–68	0	4	6	9	26	17
Total %	101	101	100	100	99	99
N	27	28	47	107	117	132

tions for left and right (see table 47). On the left, class is most often mentioned, while among Christian Democrats religion receives the greatest emphasis. Thus even when the subject is strongly ideological the two poles tend to talk past one another, emphasizing quite different dimensions and components. A generalized interest in politics, a desire and duty to participate, is mentioned by Christian Democrats but not by others. Resistance activity is an important reason for substantial minorities in all three parties, and especially for the Communists. Conventional reasons such as the influence of families and friends are cited by Socialist deputies and, to a much lesser degree, Christian Democrats; no Communist deputies mentioned these reasons.

There is considerable variation in responses depending upon when the representative joined the party. There has been an overall decline in the percentage listing ideological reasons, from 50 percent of those who joined in 1942 and before to 30 percent of those joining in 1950 and after. There is also a decline in the importance of the resistance, from 33 percent of those joining before 1943 to 12 percent of those

TABLE 47
Why Joined Party
(%)

	DEPUTIES			COUNCILORS		
	PCI	PSI-PSDI	DC	PCI	PSI-PSDI	DC
Ideology, religion, class, resistance	67	54	49	66	70	65
Family, friends, personal	0	18	6	8	7	12
Platform, issues	11	7	11	16	15	11
Other	15	21	33	10	9	12
Total %	100	100	99	100	101	100

joining after the 1940s. Issues and family and friends have increased modestly. However, it is impossible to speak very authoritatively about changing motivations since so few deputies claimed to have entered politics in recent years. For example, only four people in the deputy sample had joined their parties after the 1950s. With data from an elite level such as this we cannot meaningfully tap changes that are taking place among younger leaders within the parties: Our sample essentially represents the generation that was formed politically in the 1940s.

Previous Party Affiliations

Few of the deputies and councilors have a history of party switching, and few admit to former Fascist sympathies. Only 9 percent of the DC deputies and none from other parties mentioned Fascist party membership or sympathies. Another DC deputy had been a Monarchist. Of the DC deputies, 89 percent claimed never to have sympathized with or been members of other parties. For the PCI the figure is 93 percent, as one Communist deputy was a former DC member and another had supported *Giustizia e Libertà*, a radical movement, in his youth. However, among the Socialists there was considerable switching, as 14 percent had belonged to the Action Party and 18 percent were ex-Communists. The reason for change given by the former was of course the dissolution of the Action Party, while the ex-Communists cited their disillusionment resulting from the Hungarian invasion and the de-Stalinization campaign.

Party Offices Held

There are few ways in which party careers differ as much among the parties as in the kinds of party positions deputies have held. The most dramatic differences are between the two parties of the left, with the PCI deputies' careers reflecting a preponderance of experience at lower levels of the party's organization, while among the Socialists this experience is minimal. On the other hand, most Socialist deputies have held high office in the party, while this is not the case among the Communists. The pattern of the Christian Democrats falls between these two left parties (see table 48).

These findings undoubtedly reflect differences in the organizational structures of the various parties. The PCI and DC have much larger parliamentary delegations than the Socialists, so the same number of national officeholders in each group would result in a higher percentage for the Socialists. Equally important, however, is the PCI policy of insuring the representation in parliament of various categories of the

TABLE 48
Party Offices Held by Deputies
(% Having Held Office at that Level)

	PCI	PSI-PSDI	DC
National offices	26	82	45
Regional offices	26	7	9
Provincial offices	82	57	70
Section offices	48	7	17
N	27	28	47

party. All three parties heavily represent provincial party secretaries, with close to half having held that position. But the PCI deputies have often held other provincial-level offices as well, so that 82 percent— more than in the other two parties—have provincial-level experience. Moreover, the PCI is also experienced at the regional level, as 26 percent of its deputies claim to have held regional offices, compared with 7 percent of the Socialists and 8 percent of the Christian Democrats.

It is at the higher and lower levels that differences appear greatest. Only 7 percent of the Socialists have held section (the lowest level in the party) positions, compared with 48 percent of the Communists and 17 percent of the Christian Democrats. And holding office at the national level reflects differences that are just as dramatic—82 percent of the Socialist compared with 26 percent of the Communist and 45 percent of the DC deputies have held national office. The success of the efforts of the Communists to elevate candidates with local roots is obvious. And the difficulties that Socialist deputies have in communicating with the grassroots are also strongly suggested here. The picture of the Socialists as an elite party with weak local roots is reinforced by these data.

The success of the PCI in achieving a certain social representativeness is also reflected in the percentage of Communist deputies with experience in nonparty organizations where they work. Fully one-third of the Communists have served on union or factory committees, while none of the Socialists and only one Christian Democrat had this experience. The Socialists excelled only with youth organizations, and there the difference is minimal. None of the parties had impressive numbers of deputies with experience in women's organizations. Given the small size of our sample, we should be careful not to overinterpret small differences. On the other hand, the differences among the parties in experience at the national versus the local levels, as well as in working-class organizations, are statistically and organizationally important.

These findings reinforce the general conclusion that the Socialists, whose clientele is better educated and more sophisticated than that of the other two parties, do not rely strongly on face-to-face contacts and local organizational structures to reach their supporters. Socialist deputies are much more experienced in national and middle-level politics than at the local level; Socialist organizational weakness compared with the other two parties is also apparent here. It is less obvious, given the characteristics of Socialist voters, that this limited articulation is responsible for that party's electoral weakness. But greater presence at the local level may be necessary to enable the party to reach the mass publics attracted to the PCI and the DC.

Elective Public Offices Held

The pattern of previous public offices held reveals few major differences among the three parties, though some are worth noting. For example, 40 percent of the Christian Democratic deputies in the sample had held no other office, while the figure for the Communists is 22 percent and for the Socialists 32 percent (see table 49). The largest category for all three parties was communal councilor, with considerably more Socialists and Communists having held that position than Christian Democrats. Many within each party had served as mayor or assessor, or both, but the percentage of left deputies who had held those positions was twice as large as the percentage of Christian Democrats who had done so. The latter, on the other hand, are overrepresented among those having held some provincial elective position. This reinforces even if only slightly the general finding that Christian

TABLE 49
Elective Public Offices Held by Deputies
(In % Having Held the Office)

	PCI	PSI-PSDI	DC
Mayor	15	18	9
Assessor	19	18	9
Councilman	67	54	38
Provincial president, vice president, councilman or assessor	19	14	26
Other	0	0	9
None	22	32	40

NOTE: Figures do not add up to 100 percent because some deputies have held more than one positon.

Democratic deputies are likely to enter public life somewhat higher in the local-national hierarchy than those of other parties.

FACTIONALISM IN THE PARTY

Factionalism in Italian parties is a fascinating subject that has attracted the attention of numerous scholars.[4] The reasons for this interest are not difficult to find, for factionalism within the center and center-left parties provides the major potential for change in policies and coalitions. That is, in the absence of substantial electoral variation, the shifting balance of influence of factions and individuals provides one of the few dynamic elements in a system that seems perpetually to border on stagnation at the levels of both policy making and policy implementation. In this section we will concentrate on the part played by factions in the representatives' relationships with their parties.

Internal factionalism is important in varying degrees in all of the parties. Within the Socialist and Christian Democratic parties, election to representative organs is based on factional alignments; within the Communist party there is a de facto representation of diverse interests and points of view, which tend to become symbolized by different leaders just as in the other two parties. However, the principle of "democratic centralism" causes the Communists to deny officially that factions exist, hence Communist respondents simply refused to discuss them. There are likewise many Christian Democrats who refuse to acknowledge the existence of factions within the party. As a result, only 64 percent of the DC and none of the PCI deputies claim factional allegiance, compared with *all* of the PSI-PSDI members. Consequently, the following discussion concerns only the two groups that acknowledge factions, and data refer to our study, not official party voting statistics.

Half of the Socialists, not surprisingly, supported the majority Nenni-Mancini faction in 1968. The other half spread across a number of minority factions, with 14 percent preferring Unità e Riscossa Socialista, 11 percent DeMartino, 7 percent Giolitti, 4 percent Tanassi, 7 percent Lombardi and the left, and 7 percent the center-right or PSDI factions.

Within the DC the Dorotei, or majority faction, held the allegiance of 25 percent, which was not a majority even of the 64 percent who claimed factional ties. The next largest was Forze Nuove, with 15 percent; followed by the Nuove Cronache of Fanfani with 8 percent; Impegno Democratico of Rumor, Piccoli, and Colombo, with 6 percent; the left or *base* with 6 percent; and the center with 2 percent.

There are some differences in the perceived bases of factions within the two parties. Socialists are much more likely to emphasize ideological and policy differences, with 54 percent considering ideology as a "very important" source of factions compared with 28 percent of the DC; for policy and programmatic differences as a basis the percentages are 36 percent and 15 percent. On the other hand, there are few differences between them in the weight attributed to influential people and clientelism as a basis, with 39 percent of the PSI-PSDI and 43 percent of the DC calling this category "very important." Somewhat similar findings emerge for the representation of social interests as a basis, with 25 percent of the PSI-PSDI and 19 percent of the DC considering it very important. Internal democracy and participation were rated high by deputies of both parties; 54 percent of the PSI-PSDI and 43 percent of the DC considered these to be "very important" sources of factionalism. When asked about other influences responsible for the existence of factions, 34 percent of the DC and 18 percent of the PSI-PSDI deputies mentioned clientelism and power seeking. Also mentioned by more than two respondents were "leadership crises," "historical circumstances," and "consequences of PSI-PSDI union."

There is likewise some difference between the parties in the degree to which factions are viewed positively. While 75 percent of the Socialists approved and 4 percent were ambivalent, only 53 percent of the DC approved and 2 percent were ambivalent. The main positive reason given by both was that factions were an expression of democracy and internal differences; but the differences between the parties were substantial, with 54 percent of the PSI-PSDI and only 26 percent of the DC citing this reason. Roughly equal percentages in each party cited the importance of factions as reflecting differences of opinion and as necessary due to the large size and structural complexities of their parties. The 21 percent of the Socialists who disapproved cited divisiveness of factions, the pursuit of personal power, and the stifling of expression of opinions as the reasons for their disapproval. Christian Democrats cited the same reasons but in larger percentages.

NOMINATION AND THE CAMPAIGN

The formal aspects of nomination and election have already been discussed. At this point we take up the representative's personal perception of the process. We will concentrate on his reasons for becoming a candidate, his electioneering, and its results in terms of preference votes secured.

There is little scholarship that deals with political processes relating to nominations in Italy. This is a party matter and is not regulated by law. It is clear that in all parties it is the party as an organization that is responsible for the decision, but it is less well documented how the decisions are made. There are undoubtedly party differences in the exercise of influence. In all parties, however, there is a great deal of bargaining to achieve a "balanced" slate in the constituency. Since the constituencies are large, with up to forty-seven representatives (in Rome) in 1968, there is considerable flexibility possible in drawing up a slate; but the multiple demands are often incompatible.

An important source of difficulty is the poor match that usually exists between the electoral constituency and the organizational structure of the party. The most important organizational unit of the party is the province, while the constituencies often contain a number of provinces. In this case, the electoral lists must be hammered out between and among them. The constituency list contains a name for each seat to be filled, though it is obvious that the party is not going to get all of the votes and hence only some of the candidates will be elected. This leads to great competition for preference votes, for they determine who on the list will fill the seats to which the party is entitled by its percentage of the vote in the constituency. In other words, nomination is only a small part of the challenge of being elected. The candidate must also find ways to secure preference votes, and some organizational connection is of great assistance in this. The party is the most important source of organizational support, but its contribution varies from party to party and nowhere is it the sole source. Trade-union ties, association with Catholic Action, a carefully cultivated personal following within and without the party, or high visibility through previous public or private office are also ways used by candidates to gain preference votes. These considerations, in turn, affect the respondents' campaign strategies. We will examine what respondents have to say about this competition for preference votes later in this chapter. First, however, we will trace several chronologically prior steps.

Nominations are secured in somewhat different ways in different parties, and even within the same party there is variation from one area of the country to the other. The nomination process merits special study, but with the data at our disposal we can point out the gross outlines of party and regional differences that a specialized study could treat in finer detail.

The dominance of party organization in the parties of the left is clearly shown in the reasons given by the respondents for becoming candidates. These were open-ended questions; the responses were written down by the interviewer and coded later. They are not necessarily to be considered as adequate descriptions of empirical reality, but they undoubtedly reflect some combination of the respondents' and the parties' normative perceptions of what is proper in the nominating process. And what they show clearly is that most PCI deputies say that they became candidates because they were solicited or designated by the party; that is, they state that the initiative came from the party. Eighty percent of them gave that answer without further qualification, and an additional 8 percent gave compatible answers such as that they were nominated because of past service to the party or because the party needed someone from their province or area. Only 12 percent cited personal motivation as the reason for their candidatures.

Within the PSI-PSDI only 21 percent said that they were solicited by the party, and an additional 18 percent gave nonpersonal answers. Within the DC the comparable figures were 4 percent and 24 percent. Christian Democrats and Socialists cited such individual-oriented reasons as their role as party leaders, resistance activity, interest in politics, friends' support, the endorsement of nonparty organizations, and personal motivation.

These findings strongly suggest that for Communist deputies parliamentary activity is merely a part of a political career, undertaken because the party determined that this was the place for the militant to serve at this particular time. For the other two parties it seems to be much more central to the respondent's individual interests and needs, a personal opportunity rather than a political duty. In a sense, the office sought the Communists, while the deputies from other parties sought the office. This is not to claim that Communists are free from personal ambition and political intrigue for office; this is hardly a credible statement of human motivation. But these findings do confirm the far stronger party orientation of Communist deputies. They seem to find display of personal ambition improper, even to an anonymous interviewer.

Preference Votes

The greater role of the party organization within the Communist party is apparent when we examine the ways in which candidates go about securing preference votes. It is widely assumed among political observers that the Communist party encourages the general public to vote for the party without emphasizing individual condidates and their preference votes. In this way the determination of whom is to be elected on the PCI ticket can be left to the preference votes of the party militants, while the mass publics decide the level of PCI representation. The party makes a strong attempt to present a slate that is reasonably balanced in terms of criteria that are relevant in the constituency, such as occupational class, distinctive geographical areas, age, and sex; it is clear from the varied composition of the PCI's parliamentary delegation that it succeeds remarkably well in this. Our findings are quite consistent with the assumption of party-managed assignment of preference votes, but other explanations could also account for the findings. That is, our data support but do not necessarily confirm the contention that the PCI party organization determines who on the list will be elected by advising party activists as to how they should assign their preference votes.

Communist deputies claim not to have done much to increase their individual preference votes. We asked the respondents the following question: "In addition to presenting your party's program, what did you do to make known your qualifications for election to the Chamber and to increase your personal reputation among the voters in order to assure yourself more preference votes?" Responses were coded and then grouped into three general categories reported in table 50. Communist deputies claimed to have done very little to help themselves,

TABLE 50

Deputies' Activities to Maximize Preference Votes, by Party
(%)

	PCI	PSI-PSDI	DC
Distributed flyers, leaflets, pamphlets, articles, etc.	4	46	51
Organized or attended electoral rallies or attended meetings of party-related groups	4	21	26
Made personal contacts with voters	22	46	46

apart from personal contacts with voters, and this is in sharp contrast to the successful candidates of the other parties. Yet, PCI deputies view the party as being very helpful, especially in comparison with the other two parties as viewed by their successful candidates. The question asked was, "What does your party's organization do to assure its candidates more preference votes?" As table 51 indicates, 54 percent of the Socialists and 35 percent of the Christian Democrats in the sample said that their parties did nothing to help them, compared with only 4

TABLE 51

Party Activities to Gain Preference Votes for Deputies
(%)

	PCI	PSI-PSDI	DC
Gave indications to militants	37	4	13
Gave indications to voters	26	0	2
Issued literature on candidate	4	18	6
Organized rallies and meetings of various kinds	30	7	24
Mobilized militants in other ways	0	11	4
Party hindered candidate	0	7	15
Party did nothing to help	4	54	35
Total %	101	101	99

percent of the Communists; moreover, an additional 7 percent of the Socialists and 15 percent of the Christian Democrats—but no Communists—claimed that their party organization actually hindered them, either directly or by helping other candidates but not they themselves. Table 51 makes clear the substantial differences in the way deputies view the contributions of their party organizations. Not much should be made of the distinction between militants and voters, as the question was coded "voters" when no specific mention was made of party militants. It is possible, and indeed likely considering what we know of the electoral process from other sources, that many of the Communists coded in the "gave indications to voters" category in fact had the party's militants, who are of course also voters, in mind. The large differences between PCI deputies and others in assigning an important role to the party is further evidence of the dominance of the party organization in that party's electoral tactics.

The lack of importance assigned their parties by the others is noteworthy. The relative absence of an organizational base for Socialist candidates is clear from the minor role of rallies as well as other organized activities, combined with the greater role of campaign literature. This latter probably also reflects the higher educational achievements of the modal Socialist voter.

There are likewise revealing differences between the deputies of various parties in what they considered to be "decisive" in securing preference votes. The question asked was as follows: "Here are several things that might have helped you obtain preference votes from your voters. For each of them, would you say that it was decisive, fairly important, of little importance, or not at all important?" Table 52 presents the results for the factors that were posed to the deputies: their

TABLE 52

Factors Decisive in Securing Preference Votes for Deputies, by Party
(%)

% "Decisive"	PCI	PSI-PSDI	DC
Local political activity	65	46	56
Party activists' activity	42	21	8
Reputation in local party organ-ization	50	43	43
Position on important political problems	36	36	49
Record in parliament (incumbent only)	43	53	51

past local political activity, activities on their behalf conducted by party militants, reputation in local party organization, position on important political problems, and, for incumbent deputies, their record in parliament. The most important differences among the parties concerned the role of party activists; twice the percentage of Communists mentioned this as did Socialists, with the Christian Democrats assigning almost no decisive importance to it. Other differences are of interest but none is as revealing as this one.

The role of the mass media in campaigning, and especially in securing preference votes, is not widely understood by students of Italian politics. Radio and television are state controlled, and their formal role is limited to a series of debates and discussions involving spokesmen for the parties represented in parliament. The regular news covers the campaign, and many observers think that undue attention is devoted to the activities of the leaders of the governing Christian Democratic party. But it is not possible to buy television or radio time for political commercials, and the national nature of programming would render usage by individual candidates largely meaningless anyway. Thus it is not surprising that even in this electronic age, no one in the sample attributed any importance to radio and television.

The press is a different story, as 68 percent of the respondents thought that it made a difference in the outcome of the elections in their constituency. There is a significant difference between the responses of PCI and DC deputies, of whom 61 percent and 62 percent respectively attributed influence to the press, and the 82 percent of the PSI-PSDI deputies who did so. There are likewise differences in whether or not they viewed the influence of the press as being exerted in support of or in opposition to particular candidates or the political parties themselves. Only 4 percent of the Communists saw it as directed at candidates, while 43 percent mentioned the party and 7 percent both. With the PSI-PSDI deputies it was 21 percent candidate, 52 percent party and 18 percent both; with the DC it was 8 percent, 32 percent, and 21 percent. The Socialist representatives also more often credited the press with helping or hurting them directly— 57 percent, compared with 18 percent of the Communists and 38 percent of the Christian Democrats. The most frequent ways in which the press intervened were through reporting candidates' speeches and commenting favorably on their qualifications. Given the small sample, the results may not survive close scrutiny, but it is worth noting that none of the reports of press influence came from the south or the islands. We now turn to the representative and his campaign.

The Campaign

In the study of representation the question, "What is represented?" is an important one. It is considered in several chapters and is brought up here as background for understanding better the pattern of campaigning. It is clear that deputies feel that they represent the nation. The question was posed as follows: "Some deputies believe that a deputy has the responsibility of representing the interests of the voters of a particular city or province, others believe that he ought to represent the interests of the whole constituency. Still others believe that a deputy is the representative of the whole country. Which of these three opinions is closest to your own?"

Each should have given a single response to the question, but 10 percent of the deputies would not restrict themselves to only one. When we include multiple responses, only three of the 102 deputies interviewed failed to mention the nation. This is clearly a shared norm of parliamentarians in all parties. Article 67 of the republican constitution states, "Every member of parliament represents the nation ... " This clear constitutional mandate renders interpretation of our findings impossible, for who would violate the constitution? But it is generally true that, from a normative perspective, Italian representatives look to the nation rather than a subunit. This is a widely shared norm that was written into the constitution; it does not derive solely from that document.

Perhaps more revealing is the pattern of campaigning. Here we find a progressive expansion of the deputies' horizons from the particular to the more universal. The question asked whether the individual's campaign covered the entire constituency or whether it was concentrated in a single province, in a particular industrial or geographical zone, or in several such restricted zones. The earlier deputies were elected to parliament, the greater the percentage that claims to campaign in the entire constituency. Thus, of those first elected in 1946, 100 percent claimed the entire constituency; for the 1948 group the corresponding figure is 87 percent; for 1953 it is 62 percent; for 1958, 47 percent; for 1963, 39 percent; and for 1968, 30 percent. This is remarkable documentation of the institutionalization of support, for by expanding his contacts and increasing his visibility the deputy gradually acquires relative independence of the party organization in the narrow sense and is freer of the constraints of local intrigue.

There was a possibility that this neat progression was an artifact of the differential length of service of people in different parties. For example, of the Communists, 44 percent were first elected in 1968, compared with 39 percent of the Socialists and 21 percent of the Christian Democrats. As the former were more likely to campaign in limited areas of the constituency, this might have confounded the results. Although we quickly run into the problem of small cell entries, it seems clear that the general pattern is replicated within each of the parties. Thus in the PSI-PSDI, the percentage claiming the entire constituency between 1946 and 1968 is 100, 100, 100, 45, and 36. The only Socialists who claimed a zone smaller than the province were two who were elected in 1968. For the PCI the percentage is 100, 0, 0 (the lone Communist from 1948 and the two from 1953 all listed the province), 44, and 8. For the DC the percentage for each parliament was 83, 71, 40, 31, and 50. The reason for this upturn in 1968 is not readily apparent. The necessity for wide visibility within the PSI-PSDI is undoubtedly related to its limited electoral power, which renders popularity in a small area an insufficient electoral base. Yet the greater use of specific zones by the PCI but not by the DC, all forty-seven of whose respondents mentioned either the constituency or a province, seems to result from the greater role of the party organization in the PCI, which makes such campaign concentration feasible. But the fact that none of the PCI deputies elected before 1963 mentioned zones smaller than the province indicates that the deputies in that party who have demonstrated their survival capacity have also developed wider contacts.

We also asked the deputies which social and professional groups they had tried to reach during the electoral campaign, and there was confirmation of the conventional wisdom plus a few surprises. The question was asked in an open-ended fashion, and more than one response was coded if given. The most frequently mentioned group in each party was workers, with 85 percent of the Communists, 75 percent of the Socialists, and 53 percent of the DC mentioning them. But, as table 53 indicates, there are some unexpected results. The low level of attention of the DC to the peasants, especially compared with the Communists, is surprising, as is the level of PCI and PSI-PSDI attention to the middle class. The DC attention to the middle agricultural group (the *coltivatori diretti*) is understandable, but the 25 percent of the Socialists mentioning upper-class or professional people (almost completely the latter in this case) was not expected. Finally, the large percentage in each party that mentioned special groups such as women and youth is impressive.

TABLE 53

Social and Professional Groups Sought Out during Campaign,
by Party
(%)

Groups Deputies Sought to Reach	PCI	PSI-PSDI	DC
Workers	85	75	53
Peasants	59	32	25
Middle class	57	64	30
Middle agricultural groups (coltivatori diretti)	7	11	30
Upper-class, professional people	7	25	17
Others (women, youth, etc.)	44	32	51

A related question asked among which social classes and professional groups were the supporters of their party concentrated in their constituencies, and the results, reported in table 54, parallel those for the previous question. The wide spread of the DC responses reflects the diversity of that party. The PSI-PSDI claims to middle-class support

TABLE 54

Deputies' Views of Which Social and Professional Groups Supported
the Party, by Party
(%)

	PCI	PSI-PSDI	DC
Workers	100	93	51
Peasants	74	54	43
Middle class	41	96	64
Middle agricultural group	7	7	28
Upper classes, professional people	4	21	21
Others (women, youth, etc.)	15	18	36

document again the middle-class orientation that party so often exhibits.

The final aspect of the campaign to be considered is the candidates' perceptions of the themes that they stressed in the campaign. This was an open-ended question that was coded in considerable detail, after which the responses were grouped. The heading of ideology includes generic references to ideology, as well as issues such as democracy, freedom, Catholicism, anti-Communism, and women's rights. Political themes deal with governmental stability, structural reform, problems of the center-left, and relations among the parties. Social themes refer to problems of the working class, poor, youth, social security, and divorce. Economic themes encompass general economic problems, economic development, employment-unemployment, economic planning, and regional development. Foreign policy themes take in general references to foreign policy, peace, Italian involvement in power blocs, and European unity.

The most common themes were the social ones, and this was true within each of the parties (see table 55). There are considerable party differences, however, with 94 percent of the PCI and only 54 percent and 60 percent of PSI-PSDI and DC, respectively, mentioning social themes; most of the PCI candidates listed problems of the poor and the working class, and no PCI deputies mentioned divorce. There are no profound party differences in the treatment of ideology, though the anti-communism of the DC is mildly evident. The differences in the treatment of political and economic themes are likewise not substantial. In the realm of foreign policy only the PCI emphasis on peace is very different from the others. Party differences are along the lines that would be predicted from the bases of support and the strengths and weaknesses of the parties.

Judging from the themes emphasized by people first elected at different times, there have been some shifts in the campaign interests of candidates. There seems to be a secular decline in emphasis on ideology, with 67 percent (caution—only two of three!) of those elected in 1946, 50 percent in 1948, 38 percent in 1953, 47 percent in 1958, 39 percent in 1963, and 30 percent in 1968 mentioning ideological themes (table not shown). The conclusions relating to pre-1958 findings are based on such limited data that they cannot be considered reliable. Political themes have certainly declined, at least since 1958. The biggest shift is in social themes, which rose from 60 percent of those first elected in 1958 to 82 percent in 1968, and in economic themes, which rose from 20 percent of the 1958 group to 54 percent of the 1968 set. Foreign policy themes declined, from a peak of 50 percent among the 1953 group who mentioned them to a mere 18 percent in 1968.

Geographical differences are substantial, but they do not follow any of the conventional lines of division in the country. It was impossible to make anything of these differences using our seven-area code because of the small number of cases involved, so we put the three northern regions together with the center and the two southern regions with the islands; this provides an N of 73 in the north and center and 29 in the south (table not shown). The north and center groups are somewhat more concerned with ideological and political themes, while the combined south and islands exhibit somewhat more interest in social and foreign policy themes. Only in the emphasis on economic themes, which were mentioned by 65 percent of the southerners against only 30 percent of the north and center, do the two areas differ in truly substantial ways. While there are few differences between north and south in Italy, the greater concern of the south with its own problems is evident: There were eleven references to the economic problems of the south, and they were all made by southern deputies.

We have demonstrated the important role of party in the process of representation in Italy as well as the existence of differences among the parties. In all Italian parties, however, the organization plays a more central role than it does, for example, in the United States. For that reason, theories of representation need to be able to assign a central role to party in those systems in which it is the key institution in the electoral process. Political careers in Italy are only possible through the party.

TABLE 55
Deputies' Campaign Themes, by Party
(%)

	PCI	PSI-PSDI	DC
Ideology			
Generic	7	14	4
Democracy, freedom, equality	15	18	13
Catholicism	0	4	4
Anticommunism	0	4	17
Women's rights	4	0	2
None of these	74	61	57
Total %	100	101	97
Political Themes			
Generic	11	7	2
Government stability	0	4	4
Problems of left	15	0	0
Problems of center-left	0	11	6
Structural reform	4	4	19
Relations among parties	0	18	6
Combinations	0	4	2
None of these	70	54	60
Total %	100	102	99
Social Themes			
Generic	4	7	8
Poor and working-class problems	67	0	8
Problems of other groups	4	4	4
Youth and school problems	4	7	19
Divorce and family questions	0	11	2
Combinations	15	25	19
None of these	7	46	38
Total %	101	100	98
Economic Themes			
Generic	4	7	17
Work	7	4	0
Economic development	7	0	4
Regional development	7	4	4
Economic planning	4	7	2
Problems of south	15	11	8
Combinations	0	4	0
Agricultural development	0	4	4
None of above	56	64	60
Total %	100	101	99
Foreign Policy			
Generic	7	11	4
Peace	22	4	2
NATO, power blocs	4	0	2
European unity, Common Market	0	4	2
Combinations and other	15	4	6
None of these	52	79	83
Total %	100	102	99

10

Representation in Italy
—and Beyond

This research on representation in Italy began with assumptions about elite-mass linkages that emerged primarily from the empirical study of American politics and that in turn derived from the Anglo-American tradition of thinking about representation. The research design focused on the relationship between the policy preferences of elite and mass in geographically based constituencies and on their perceptions of that relationship. This is a design that can be utilized in any country with free elections, and it is certainly appropriate for Italy. However, our research indicates that data obtained by means of this design must be interpreted within the context of a broader theoretical framework if we are to maximize our understanding of the nature of representation.

As a contribution to the construction of that framework we have suggested several conceptual innovations. We have argued that representation can best be viewed as a dimension of mobilization—the normative dimension—and, consequently, that theories of representation must be developed concurrently with theories of mobilization. As the normative or evaluative dimension of mobilization, representation refers to the *quality* of the elite-mass linkages in a society, and, in this area as in others, quality lies in large part in the eyes of the beholder. But, as in other areas of life, there are reasonably good indicators of quality even if no agreement is ultimately possible as to which indicator is the proper one. That is, the fit between elite and mass on social isomorphism, policy preferences, basic beliefs, and perceived commonality of

156

material interests can be measured rather satisfactorily, though people will continue to differ as to the relative weight that should be given each of these criteria. That is why we label representation the normative dimension of mobilization and why we do not expect consensus as to the representativeness of any particular set of political institutions and processes.

Mobilization incorporates participation, but it is far more than that. For participation involves some active effort on the part of the individual, whereas mobilization refers to the establishment of elite-mass linkages whether there is overtly political activity involved or not. This distinction is especially important in Italy, where many people are caught up in politics through no particular effort of their own. The Church, for example, does a very effective job of electoral mobilization of the religiously motivated citizens whether there is any *political* interest or *political* participation involved or not, and the same could be said for other categories of people and organizations. In this way, broader societal structures are brought into politics and the significance of representation is enhanced, for it comes to involve ways of living as well as policy preferences on the issues of the day.

The realization that representation in Italy involved so much more than these contemporary policy preferences led us to view political traditions as the link between the larger issues and the specific parliamentary vote. These traditions, institutionalized in the very structure of the society and with the parties as their principal political arms, are much more important than their particular political manifestation at any one time or place. Because of the strength of the traditions within societal institutions, they are quite effective in perpetuating themselves and in forcing new forms of cleavage into the existing channels of politics. And while the parties are the dominant political structures, the traditions extend far beyond the boundaries of the party. Moreover, the traditions are not coterminous with ideologies, subcultures, classes, or interests, though they certainly reflect disproportionately the distribution of these lines of cleavage within the Italian population. The parties and the traditions thus mobilize an impressive portion of the population into stable patterns of partisanship. Yet this does not lead to effective government and a contented population. While we do not think that we have explained the reasons for the political malaise that is widely felt in Italy, we can contribute to a better understanding of it through this analysis of representation.

It should be noted that the extensive mobilization achieved by the parties is largely electoral mobilization only. Turnout in elections is very high in comparison with other liberal democracies; furthermore, four-fifths of those who vote claim to have always voted for the same party. Our research and that of others indicate that there is little crossing of the boundaries separating the major traditions. As a consequence, the heavily mobilized electorate shifts its votes very little from election to election, so that elections do not serve effectively as a device for rewarding and punishing incumbents and opposition. Indeed, governmental performance has little direct impact on electoral outcomes. The major source of electoral change seems to be the marginal differences in partisan preferences between those entering the electorate through coming of age and those leaving it through death.

The absence of significant electoral change need not be incompatible with effective control over parties. But if elections are not a realistic means of discipline, some functional equivalent must exist. This could take the form of a lively internal party life, in which an active party democracy controls elites and continually revitalizes the internal political process. A vast literature attests to the rarity of the achievement of internal party democracy.[1] It certainly does not exist within the Christian democratic party, which, because of its size and position, is the most important for Italian policymaking.

The result is—to use the concepts of Hirschman—that Italian citizens exercise neither exit nor voice in that most important of political institutions, the dominant party. That is, they have neither abandoned it when quality declines nor become active in order to improve it.[2] The result is recurring problems of loyalty, in which actions denote continued loyalty to the tradition while leaving the question in doubt concerning political institutions. Since the traditions are only in part political, political malaise is not sufficient to destroy loyalty to the tradition; but it does weaken support for political institutions. And it should be repeated that this is most relevant within the Christian Democratic party itself.

Mobilization is more electoral than organizational, and, in part for that very reason, it is only in part political. For the importance of the traditions and of nonparty organizations brings into politics many concerns that go beyond the narrow issues of day-to-day decision making. Of course, everything is potentially political; we are not arguing that ideology and revolution, for example, are not important political issues. But they are issues that are not likely to be put to rest in a generally satisfactory manner by any government in a pluralist democracy; no matter what is done, dissatisfaction is likely to result, for the demands are incompatible and irreconcilable. In Italy the basic cultural assumptions of a badly divided society are fed into the political process for debate and resolution. But these questions are never resolved, because no solution is generally acceptable. Elites must come up with workable solutions even without a societal consensus. Few of the basic questions that have surfaced in the history of modern Italy have really been confronted and disposed of. In the postwar period only the question of the disposition of the monarchy and—perhaps— the right to divorce have been laid to rest; and both were accomplished in an extraordinary manner through the popular referendum and not by the normal political process.

The result is that much of political debate is unrelated to governmental outputs. We have seen that the issues dividing the parties are substantial; we have also shown that the concerns of mass publics are not grossly dissimilar across the parties. Electoral politics is a civic drama of a classical kind, designed to entertain and educate, but having little impact on outputs of the system.

Outputs emerge from another game, one that is as pragmatic and personalistic as the electoral game is ideological and party related. This policy game has little relationship with the electoral game. The latter determines who can play the former; it has little to do with who wins or loses. And since elections result in little change in the identity of the players, the practical impact of elections on policy outcomes has in the past been limited.

Our study of electoral representation in Italy is finished; the study of representation in Italy is only half complete, however, for there is another side of representation that we have barely touched upon. If representation is the evaluative component of elite-mass linkages, then these linkages must be studied wherever they take place. And in Italy it is clear that in the past administrative and clientelistic ties have been as important in developing elite-mass linkages as elections and party organizations. It is equally clear that representation in the informal Italian governmental process is far from the one-person, one-vote ideal of democratic theory. Ties to the Catholic tradition, economic and social position, and personalistic contacts are the principal determinants of access in this game. We have suggested some of the ways in which representation takes place in the informal government, through individual and group involvement in the decision-making process. But our research design, deriving as it does from a concern with electoral representation, does not permit us to travel very far down that road.

A general observation based on the study of the electoral side does seem quite relevant for understanding the functioning of the system.

The electoral game focuses on the large issues that are not easily dealt with in any polity; the policy game, by restricting the players to a more compatible set, functions in a very pragmatic and ad hoc manner. Only parties and parliament can formulate long-range policy; only a pragmatic informal politics can compensate for their inability to do so. But the result is an absence of coherence in policy, extreme inequalities in access to the values achievable through politics, and widespread frustration and disillusionment with government and politics.

Yet this malaise is hardly reflected in the electoral game. Mass publics continue to support their traditions and the parties that represent them in politics. In fact, Italy has been very successful in maintaining an equitable system of electoral representation. Fraud is virtually nonexistent, turnout remains among the highest in the world, the distribution of parliamentary seats closely reflects the division of the popular vote—whatever criteria are employed, the Italian electoral system functions well.

But electoral representation is only part of the process of representation. Analysis of other aspects of representation is largely outside the scope of this study, yet it is crucial to a complete understanding of the subject. We began with a research design that would maximize our understanding of electoral aspects of representation. Other designs are necessary for the study of informal aspects of representation. We are content to have contributed to the understanding of electoral representation in Italy and to the elaboration of a new conceptual framework for the study of representation.

APPENDIX

The Design of the Study

This study of representation in Italy focuses on political attitudes and behaviors at the mass and elite levels at the time of the 1968 national parliamentary elections and is based on three national surveys administered in that year. In the first of these, 2,500 respondents were interviewed from a representative stratified national sample; in the second, 386 municipal councilors were interviewed in a national sample of communes; in the third, 103 deputies elected in May of that year were interviewed. The three samples thus provide a mass and two elite levels for analysis, and they make possible and appropriate the operationalization of representation adopted in this study.

Italian political traditions find institutionalization in religious organizations, trade unions, business and industrial enterprises, and bureaucracies as well as political parties. The party serves as the principal political arm of the tradition, and it is consequently the party that receives the bulk of attention, but it must be kept in mind that other institutions are likewise important. This study focuses on representatives and the represented and the linkages between them. It also examines the similarities and differences between the several political traditions. It focuses on a specific point in time and relies heavily on data gathered during an election period, but it is as concerned with representation as with electoral behavior, with linkages as with partisan choice.

The reasons for this emphasis on linkage are central to the assumptions on which this study is based, and these assumptions, in turn, rest upon the conviction that ties to party, which is the political component of the tradition, are what are most important in Italian electoral politics. National elections are not so much measures of the ability of particular individuals, parties, and programs to appeal to the electorate in the space of a short campaign as they are the registration of what secular trends in mortality and modernization are doing to particular political traditions. There are changes in the fortunes of parties from one election to another, to be sure, but they are seldom primarily the result of the campaign itself and have never been dramatic from one election to another.

In the period since the Second World War and up to and including the 1968 election, mass partisanship in Italy has been strongly anchored in the social networks of the left and of the Church. A study of representation consequently must pay attention to these networks. Indeed, the analysis of electoral choice in Italy must incorporate these ties and hence must focus on more than the act of voting itself: It must focus on the total process of representation of which voting is merely a part.

As mentioned previously, the problem of representation—the meaning of the concept—can be analyzed on several levels. But to accept the possibility of various levels of analysis is not to demonstrate their existence among mass publics. Sophistication is rare at the mass level. Mass publics certainly possess preferences among alternatives, opinions (at least on subjects that are salient for them), affect toward persons and objects relevant to politics, and satisfaction and dissatisfaction with what goes on in the political system; but most people do not view politics at a very high level of abstraction. Although the higher abstractions of philosophy may be read into their outlooks, their own belief systems are likely to reflect a concern with the concrete, the specific, the here and now. As this study is concerned with the linkage between mass publics and elites, it is necessary to concentrate on what is relevant to both, which in the present study means operationalizing problems at the less complex level of mass publics. As a result, this study aims at a level of sophistication in the treatment of attitudes and ideologies that is lower than would be proper if it dealt only with elites. In the operationalization of the concept of representation it concentrates on the lowest common denominators. It is obvious that there are more complex and sophisticated ways of posing questions, coding responses, and attacking methodological problems. However, by limiting the level of sophistication to what can be dealt with using a methodology appropriate to the study of mass publics, it is possible to relate mass opinion and behavior to those of elites of two types and at two levels.

The Study Design

The present study is a part of the program in comparative studies in representation carried out by political scientists at the University of Michigan and made possible by a Ford Foundation grant for international programs at the University. These studies embody a commitment to the analysis of national samples of mass publics and of members of the lower house of the national legislatures. Insofar as is compatible with the substantive problems of studying representation in a variety of settings, these studies are similar in the dimensions probed, the questions asked, and the measures employed. They have been executed in Australia, France, Germany, Italy, Japan, the Netherlands, Sweden, the United Kingdom, and the United States. Although they were designed to facilitate eventual cross-national analyses, each country study stands alone.

In some of the countries several areas of inquiry were investigated for the first time. So little is known of a systematic nature about the subject of representation in some countries that the studies had to be very general; in others, previous work had mapped out the terrain and made possible more focused inquiry. Italy in 1968 fell between the two extremes. A great deal of valuable research had been carried out on Italian politics; little, however, had dealt with mass publics and the problem of representation. In fact, there had been little systematic inquiry at the national level utilizing sample surveys. What had been done was limited to market research for commercial purposes and, when political in subject matter, dealt with questions concerning voting intentions, orientations toward politicians and policies, and so on. More theoretically oriented surveys carried out under academic auspices were mainly limited in geographical scope and theoretical import. A notable exception is the *Civic Culture* study of Gabriel Almond and Sidney Verba, which had been executed a decade previous to the present survey.

The design of the present study is simple and straightforward. The study is based on three surveys that are national in scope (with the reservations explained below) and that are designed to give comparable measures on a number of variables related to representation from three different populations. These are samples of mass publics, of communal councilors, and of deputies.

The national sample was of 3,000 respondents, of whom 2,500 were interviewed for a response rate of 83.3 percent. It was executed in June and July of 1968, following the parliamentary elections of May 19–20, 1968, by CISER (Centro Italiano di Studi e Ricerche) of Rome under the direction of Sergio Lieto. The sample was drawn from lists of voters in electoral precincts in a national sample of communes. To obtain the sample of communes, all Italian communes were stratified by the area of the country they were in and by their size, and an equal number was selected from each category. The number of respondents in each commune was proportionate to the commune's contribution to the total national population. The sample thus provides a representative sample of the entire electorate.

The other two samples include representatives from the three most important parties at the time of the 1968 election—the Communists, the Socialists (at that time the unified Partito Socialista Italiano and the Partito Social Democratico Italiano, or PSI-PSDI), and the Christian Democratic party. These parties among them received 81.5 percent of the votes in the 1968 elections to the Chamber of Deputies and 84.6 percent of the seats. They likewise dominate local politics in the country as a whole, though other parties have pockets of local strength. The lack of overall national strength on the part of the other parties combined with their number—ten parties were represented in the legislature—suggested a research strategy that would maximize the comparability of the major parties at the expense of the minor ones.

The interviews with communal councilors were administered first, in April of 1968. These were carried out in a subsample of seventy-five of the 300 communes used in the national mass sample and thus are a representative national sample of communes. Interviewers were given a quota of two Communists, two Socialists, and two Christian Democrats within each commune; where relevant and possible, these were to include the mayor, vice-mayor, and leader of the opposition. These instructions were not followed to the letter, with the result that only thirty-six mayors, thirty-six vice-mayors, and twenty-two leaders of the opposition were interviewed. A total of 450 councilors should have been interviewed, but only 400 interviews were obtained; fourteen of these had to be discarded because they were with independents or members of parties outside the sample, so the number of utilizable interviews is 386. Because of the sampling procedures employed, this may be considered a representative sample of communes but not of councilors.

The sample of deputies likewise includes only members of the Communist, Socialist, and Christian Democratic parties elected or reelected in May of 1968. These were sampled randomly from a list of the deputies. We considered matching the deputies with the sampling points of the mass sample, but a system of proportional representation and large constituencies makes that less appealing than in the United States or the United Kingdom. Moreover, the sampling procedures used for the mass survey insure that there are respondents in most of the constituencies. In addition, the uneven distribution of deputies by party across the constituencies would have made it difficult to maximize the payoff from that type of design. Finally, proportional representation made it seem unwise, in a study with limited resources, to plan to interview unsuccessful candidates as was done in several other countries in the project.

The deputies interviewed are a good sample of the deputies of the three major parties. Our sample of 132 deputies was obtained by selecting every fourth deputy in the three major parties; 103 of these were interviewed in the latter half of 1968 by experienced interviewers of the staff of CISER.

Notes

NOTES TO CHAPTER ONE

1. Gerhard Loewenberg, "The Role of Parliaments in Modern Political Systems," in Loewenberg, ed., *Modern Parliaments: Change or Decline* (Chicago: Aldine-Atherton, 1971), p. 3.

2. For an example of this level of analysis see Eric Vogelin, *The New Science of Politics* (Chicago: University of Chicago Press, 1952).

3. Introductions to this tradition of analysis include Anthony H. Birch, *Representation* (New York: Praeger, 1971); J. Roland Pennock and John W. Chapman, eds., *Representation: Nomos X* (New York: Atherton, 1968); and Hannah Pitkin, *The Concept of Representation* (Berkeley: University of California Press, 1967).

4. The literature dealing with this dimension is voluminous and will be cited only in specific contexts.

5. Alfred de Grazia, "Representation-Theory," *International Encyclopedia of the Social Sciences*, 13:461.

6. Giovanni Sartori, "Representational Systems," *International Encyclopedia of the Social Sciences*, 13:471, 473.

7. Heinz Eulau and Kenneth Prewitt, *Labyrinths of Democracy: Adaptations, Linkages, Representation, and Policies in Urban Politics* (Indianapolis: Bobbs-Merrill, 1973), pp. 22–23. See also Prewitt and Eulau, "Political Matrix and Political Representation: Prolegomenon to a New Departure from an Old Problem," *American Political Science Review* 63 (June 1969): 427–41; and Eulau, "Changing Views of Representation," *Micro-Macro Political Analysis: Accents of Inquiry* (Chicago: Aldine, 1969), pp. 76–102.

8. *Labyrinths*, p. 23.

9. Numerous scholars have contributed to a vast literature on mobilization. For an overview of this field see J. P. Nettl, *Political Mobilization* (New York: Basic Books, 1967).

10. See chap. 14 in Samuel H. Barnes, *Party Democracy: Politics in an Italian Socialist Federation* (New Haven, Conn.: Yale University Press, 1967), pp. 234–55. These themes are developed further in Barnes, "Mobilitazione e conflitto politico," *Rassegna italiana di sociologia* 8 (October–December 1967): 503–24.

11. Thus Sidney Verba, Norman H. Nie, and Jae-on Kim write, "By political participation we refer to all those activities by private citizens that are more or less directly aimed at influencing the selection of governmental personnel and/or the decisions that they make." *The Modes of Democratic Participation: A Cross-National Comparison* (Beverly Hills, Calif.: Sage, 1971), p. 9. See also Lester W. Milbrath, *Political Participation* (Chicago: Rand McNally, 1965); and Sidney Verba and Norman Nie, *Participation in America* (New York: Harper and Row, 1972).

12. There is an immense literature on cleavages and conflict. A method for formalizing their analysis is presented in Douglas W. Rae and Michael Taylor, *The Analysis of Political Cleavages* (New Haven, Conn.: Yale University Press, 1970). Analyses of cleavage structures in Western democracies are included in Richard Rose, ed., *Electoral Behavior: A Comparative Handbook* (New York: Free Press, 1974); this volume contains extensive bibliographies on each of the countries discussed. See also S. M. Lipset and Stein Rokkan, "Cleavage Structures, Party Systems, and Voter Alignments: An Introduction," in Lipset and Rokkan, eds., *Party Systems and Voter Alignments: Cross-National Perspectives* (New York: Free Press, 1967), pp. 1–64.

13. The impact of electoral laws is analyzed in Douglas W. Rae, *The Political Consequences of Electoral Laws* (New Haven, Conn.: Yale University Press, 1967).

14. Robert D. Putnam, *The Comparative Study of Political Elites* (Englewood Cliffs, N.J.: Prentice-Hall, 1976), p. 163.

15. Nelson W. Polsby reaches similar conclusions: "Strong and deep-rooted traditions of citizen noninvolvement in political decision making and social deference associated with near-feudal social stratification systems appear to be necessary for the maintenance of large-scale societies for any greater length of time without a significant movement toward legitimization processes that are more representative, explicitly consent-oriented, and hence more legislative in character" ("Legislatures," in Polsby and Fred I. Greenstein, eds., *Handbook of Political Science*, Reading, Mass., Addison-Wesley, 1975, vol. 5, p. 265).

16. A sampling of this literature relevant for our purposes would include the following: William D. Schorger and Eric R. Wolf, eds., *Social and Political Processes in the Western Mediterranean*, a special issue of the *Anthropology Quarterly* 42 (July 1969); Michael Banton, ed., *The Social Anthropology of Complex Societies* (London: Tavistock, 1966); Julian Pitt-Rivers, *The People of the Sierra* (Chicago: Univ. of Chicago Press, 1961); Sidney Tarrow, *Peasant Communism in Southern Italy* (New Haven, Conn.: Yale University Press, 1967), pp. 40–95; Jack M. Potter, May N. Diaz, and George Foster, eds., *Peasant Society: A Reader* (Boston: Little, Brown, & Co., 1967); Edward Banfield, *The Moral Basis of a Backward Society* (Glencoe, Ill.: Free Press, 1958); René Lemarchand and Keith Legg, "Political Clientelism and Development," *Comparative Politics* 4 (January 1972): 149–78; René Lemarchand, "Political Clientelism and Ethnicity in Tropical Africa: Competing Solidarities in

Nation-Building," *American Political Science Review* 66 (March 1972): 68–90; James C. Scott, "Patron-Client Politics and Political Change in Southeast Asia," *American Political Science Review* 66 (March 1972): 91–113; Luigi Graziano, "Patron-Client Relationships in Southern Italy," *European Journal of Political Research* 1 (April 1973): 3–34; Johan Galtung, *Members of Two Worlds* (New York: Columbia University Press, 1971).

17. Tarrow, p. 74.

18. Ibid.

19. Alan Zuckerman, "Political Cleavage: A Conceptual and Theoretical Analysis," *British Journal of Political Science* 5 (April 1975): 242; see also Zuckerman, "Social Structure and Political Competition: The Italian Case," *World Politics* 24 (April 1972): 428–44; and Zuckerman, *Political Clienteles in Power: Party Factions and Cabinet Coalitions in Italy*, Sage Professional Papers in Comparative Politics, 01–055 (Beverly Hills, Calif.: Sage, 1975).

20. Zuckerman, "Political Cleavage."

21. In their seminal work on participation, Sidney Verba and Norman Nie note some of the consequences in America of particularistic contacts, which are close to the patterns we are describing here. They found that they were the only form of participation without high relationships with several other modes of activity (*Participation in America*, p. 77).

22. Banfield, p. 85.

23. Writing about the effects of this kind of politics in Iran, James A. Bill notes that "genuine participation and deep political institutionalization are not necessarily advanced by legislative bodies. Legislatures can serve as instruments that subtly impede change and preserve patterns of oppression and repression;" in "The Politics of Legislative Monarchy: The Iranian Majlis," in Herbert Hirsch and M. Donald Hancock, eds., *Comparative Legislative Systems* (New York: Free Press, 1971), p. 369. Richard A. Styskal found that representatives in the Philippine legislature relied heavily upon patron-client types of ties, though he avoids our terminology. Instead, he speaks of traditional and modern forms of political action, equating these in a rough fashion with "unattached individuals" and "interest groups" as actors in the system ("Philippine Legislators' Reception of Individuals and Interest Groups in the Legislative Process," in Hirsch and Hancock, p. 60).

24. This seems evident in several studies dealing with diverse systems: Hirsch and Hancock; Allan Kornberg, ed., *Legislatures in Comparative Perspective* (New York: McKay, 1973); Allan Kornberg and Lloyd Musolf, eds., *Legislatures in Developmental Perspective* (Durham, N.C.: Duke University Press, 1970); and Gerhard Loewenberg, ed., *Modern Parliaments: Change or Decline* (Chicago: Aldine-Atherton, 1971).

25. This process has been analyzed by Hans Daalder, "Parties, Elites, and Political Developments in Western Europe," in Joseph LaPalombara and Myron Weiner, eds., *Political Parties and Political Development* (Princeton, N.J.: Princeton University Press, 1966); Robert T. Holt and John E. Turner, *The Political Basis of Economic Development* (Princeton, N.J.: D Van Nostrand, 1966); Samuel P. Huntington, *Political Order in Changing Societies* (New Haven, Conn.: Yale University Press, 1968); Barrington Moore, Jr., *The Social Origins of Dictatorship and Democracy* (Boston: Beacon, 1966).

26. *Party Systems.*

27. Apart from Warren E. Miller and Donald E. Stokes, to whom we owe a special intellectual and personal debt, and who are cited in the pages that follow, we wish here to acknowledge our debt to several researchers in this tradition: J. D. Barber, *The Lawmakers* (New Haven, Conn.: Yale University Press, 1965); Jean Blondel, *Comparative Legislatures* (Englewood Cliffs, N.J.: Prentice-Hall, Inc., 1973); Morris P. Fiorina, *Representatives, Roll Calls, and Constituencies* (Lexington, Mass.: Lexington Books, 1974); Malcolm E. Jewell and Samuel C. Patterson, *The Legislative Process in the United States* (New York: Random House, 1966); Allan Kornberg, *Canadian Legislative Behavior* (New York: Holt, Rinehart & Winston, 1967); Gerhard Loewenberg, *Parliament in the German Political System* (Ithaca, N.Y.: Cornell University Press, 1967); Duncan MacRae, Jr., *Parliament, Parties, and Society in France, 1946–1958* (New York: St. Martin's, 1967); Nelson W. Polsby, "The Institutionalization of the U.S. House of Representatives," *American Political Science Review* 62 (March 1968): 144–68; Austin Ranney, *Pathways to Parliament* (Madison: University of Wisconsin Press, 1965); Wayne Shannon, *Party Constituency and Congressional Voting* (Baton Rouge: Louisiana State University Press, 1968); Julius Turner, *Party and Constituency: Pressures on Congress* (Baltimore: Johns Hopkins Press, 1951); J. C. Wahlke, H. Eulau, H. Buchanan, and LeRoy Ferguson, *The Legislative System* (New York: Wiley, 1962).

28. Loewenberg, "The Role of Parliaments," pp. 15–16.

29. Warren E. Miller and Donald E. Stokes, "Constituency Influence in Congress," *American Political Science Review* 57 (March 1963): pp. 45–56.

30. Giovanni Sartori, "Introductory Report," Roundtable Meeting on Parliamentary Government, Bellagio, 1963; cited in Allan Kornberg, "Parliament in Canadian Society," in Kornberg and Musolf, p. 84.

31. Heinz Eulau and Katherine Hinckley, "Legislative Institutions and Processes," in James A. Robinson, ed., *Political Science Annual* (Indianapolis: Bobbs-Merrill, 1966), 1:85–189.

32. Giuseppe DiPalma analyzes the policy game in his *Surviving Without Governing: The Italian Parties in Parliament* (Berkeley and Los Angeles: University of California Press, 1977).

33. We are aware that a substantial body of literature questions the relationship between public policy and variables relating to representation, especially in the American states. For a review of these findings, see Thomas R. Dye, *Politics, Economics, and the Public: Policy Outcomes in the American States* (Chicago: Rand McNally, 1966); Richard I. Hofferbert, "The Relation between Public Policy and Some Structural and Environmental Variables in the American States," *American Political Science Review* 60 (March 1966): 73–82, and *The Study of Public Policy* (Indianapolis: Bobbs-Merrill, 1974). For an extension of this type of analysis to other countries, see Philips Cutright, "Political Structure, Economic Development, and National Security Programs," *American Journal of Sociology* 70 (March 1965): 537–48.

34. That is, insofar as voting and the counting of ballots are concerned. The clientelistic practices employed by several parties often involve the virtual buying of votes, but this is accomplished before the vote enters the formal electoral process.

35. Joseph LaPalombara develops the distinction between *clientela* and

parentela relationships in his *Interest Groups in Italian Politics* (Princeton, N.J.: Princeton University Press, 1963).

36. Giorgio Galli defines *sottogoverno* as "the sum of all the offices, of all the centers of power, of all the positions whose assignment in Italy depend on the executive." *Il bipartitismo imperfetto* (Bologna: Il Mulino, 1966), p. 198. The functioning of the *sottogoverno* in Italy is a common topic of conversation and speculation but, for obvious reasons, there is little empirical scholarly evidence about it. Widespread bribery of officials, abuse of police and intelligence powers, clerical and other interference in administrative matters, and almost universal politicization in a partisan manner of virtually all aspects of life touched by the state are documented by court trials, exposés, journalistic accounts, and daily life in Italy.

37. Verba and Nie point out that this mode of participation, which they label "citizen-initiated contacts," is less related to a general dimension of participation than were the other modes. It seems, in a sense, to be a different game. For the United States, see Verba and Nie, *Participation in America;* for the cross-national study, Verba, Nie, and Kim, *The Modes of Democratic Participation,* p. 63. They note further that "contacting on a narrow personal issue stands at one extreme of that dimension [scope of outcome] and it has no relationship to general political activity. This is a very distinctive type of political participation, a type we might somewhat paradoxically call *parochial participation*—borrowing the term from Almond and Verba, who use it to identify citizens who lack any positive orientation toward public life" (*Participation in America,* pp. 68–69; italics in original).

38. On this point see Giorgio Galli and Alfonso Prandi, *Patterns of Political Participation in Italy* (New Haven, Conn.: Yale University Press, 1970), pp. 255–301; Pierre Ferrari and Herbert Maisl, *Les Groupes communistes aux assemblées parlementaires italiennes (1958–1963) et françaises (1962–1967)* (Paris: Presses Universitaires de France, 1969); Franco Cazzola, "Consenso e opposizione nel parlamento italiano: il ruolo del PCI dalla I alla IV legislatura," *Rivista italiano di scienza politica* 2 (April 1972): 71–96; and DiPalma, *Surviving Without Governing.*

39. The late Giuseppe Maranini developed the concept of *partitocrazia:* In several books, he argued that Italy is ruled by party leaders responsible only to their own organizations rather than to the electorate as a whole; they function outside of the parliamentary process, so that decisions are not made in parliament as required by the constitution. His argument reinforces our contention that the electoral process and the policy process intersect only slightly in Italy. However, we also emphasize the importance of organizations other than parties; we think that the *partitocrazia* argument elevates parties at the expense of other organizations in the policy process, suggesting that parties have an autonomy from other social forces that they do not in fact possess. Maranini, *Miti e realtà della democrazia* (Milano: Comunità, 1958), and *La costituzione che dobbiamo salvare* (Milano: Comunità, 1961).

40. Eulau and Prewitt, (see n. 7 above).

41. Gerhard Loewenberg, "The Institutionalization of Parliament and Public Orientations of the Political System," in Kornberg, ed., *Legislatures in Comparative Perspective*, pp. 142–56; see also John C. Wahlke, "Policy De-

mands and System Support: The Role of the Represented," in Loewenberg, ed., *Modern Parliaments*, pp. 141–71.

42. Martin O. Heisler, in collaboration with Robert B. Kvavik, carries the thrust of Loewenberg's analysis even further, arguing that the "European Polity" model rests upon three classes of phenomena: (1) the decreasing importance of input-side activity in political life, especially as it influences the content and focus of public policy; (2) the growing importance of structural parameters as the major determinants of activity in and orientations toward the authorities and the regime; and (3) the increased political importance of administration in everyday life, with administration viewed broadly, as the processes and structures involved in the implementation of outputs" in Heisler and Kvavik, "Patterns of European Politics: The 'European Polity' Model," in Heisler, ed., *Politics in Europe* [New York: David McKay, 1974], p. 36). While Italy exhibits these phenomena in varying degrees, it does not, in our opinion (and probably in Heisler's as well), follow the "European Polity" model in incorporating all groups into the decision-making process (Heisler, p. 49). La Palombara has described how Italian politics systematically excludes groups lacking a *parentela* relationship with the ruling party or parties.

43. Galli and Prandi, p. 257.

44. "Constituency Influence in Congress;" also, "Representation in the American Congress," manuscript (Ann Arbor, Mich.: Center for Political Studies). See also Stokes and Miller, "Party Government and the Saliency of Congress," *Public Opinion Quarterly* 26 (Winter 1962): 531–46; and Miller, "Majority Rule and the Representative System of Government," in Erik Allardt and Y. Littunen, eds., *Ideologies and Party Systems* (Helsinki: Transactions of the Westermarck Society, 1964), pp. 343–76; repr. in Allardt and Stein Rokkan, eds., *Mass Politics* (New York: Free Press, 1970), pp. 284–311.

NOTES TO CHAPTER TWO

1. The quotation is from Samuel P. Huntington, *Political Order in Changing Societies* (New Haven, Conn.: Yale University Press, 1968), p. 12.

2. Although the family is of course a very important "institution," at this point our focus is not the individual level; we will reserve our discussion of the family until later.

3. Considering its importance in Italian public life there are remarkably few scholarly studies of the Church in Italian politics. The following will serve as an introduction: Arturo Carlo Jemolo, *Church and State in Italy: 1850–1950* (Oxford: Blackwell, 1960); Alfonso Prandi, *Chiesa e politica* (Bologna: Il Mulino, 1968); Domenico Settembrini, *La chiesa nella politica italiana 1949–1963* (Pisa: Nistri-Lischi, 1964); Richard A. Webster, *The Cross and the Fasces: Christian Democracy and Fascism in Italy* (Stanford, Calif.: Stanford University Press, 1960); and Gianfranco Poggi, *Catholic Action in Italy: The Sociology of a Sponsored Organization* (Stanford, Calif.: Stanford University Press, 1967); Carlo Falconi, *La chiesa e le organizzazioni cattoliche in Italia (1945–1955)* (Turin: Einaudi, 1956).

4. On some of these institutions, see LaPalombara, (chap. 1, n. 35), and *The Italian Labor Movement* (Ithaca, N.Y.: Cornell University Press, 1957); D. L. Horowitz, *The Italian Labor Movement* (Cambridge, Mass.: Harvard University Press, 1963); Jean Meynaud and Claudio Risé, *Gruppi di pressione in Italia*

e in Francia (Naples: ESI, 1963); Agopik Manoukian, ed., *La presenza sociale del PCI e della DC* (Bologna: Il Mulino, 1968); and Galli and Prandi (chap. 1, n. 38).

5. For examples of these findings, see Gabriel Almond and Sidney Verba, *The Civic Culture* (Princeton, N.J.: Princeton University Press, 1963); and Samuel H. Barnes, "Italy: Religion and Class in Electoral Behavior," in Rose (chap. 1, n. 12), pp. 171–225.

6. Hans Daalder, "The Consociational Democracy Theme," *World Politics* 26 (July 1974): 611.

7. Huntington, p. 12.

8. Arend Lijphart, *The Politics of Accommodation: Pluralism and Democracy in the Netherlands* (Berkeley: University of California Press, 1968), and "Consociational Democracy," *World Politics* 21 (January 1969): 207–25.

9. Val Lorwin, "Segmented Pluralism: Ideological Cleavages and Political Cohesion in the Smaller European Democracies," *Comparative Politics* 3 (January 1971): 141–75.

10. Jürg Steiner, *Amicable Agreement versus Majority Rule: Conflict Resolution in Switzerland* (Chapel Hill: University of North Carolina Press, 1974).

11. Gerhard Lehmbruch, *Proporzdemokratie: Politisches System und Politische Kultur in der Schweiz und in Oesterreich* (Tübingen: Mohr, 1967).

12. See also Daalder; Kenneth MacRae, ed., *Consociational Democracy: Political Accommodation in Segmented Societies* (Toronto: McClelland & Stewart, 1974); and G. Bingham Powell, Jr., *Social Fragmentation and Political Hostility: An Austrian Case Study*, (Stanford, Calif.: Stanford University Press, 1970).

13. Gianfranco Pasquino, "Il sistema politico italiano tra neo-trasformismo e democrazia consociative," *Il mulino* 22 (July–August 1973): 549–66; Samuel H. Barnes, "The Dark Side of Pluralism: Italian Democracy and the Limits of Political Engineering," in John H. Hallowell, ed., *Prospects for Constitutional Democracy* (Durham, N.C.: Duke University Press, 1976), pp. 75–100.

14. Nelson W. Polsby, "The Institutionalization of the U.S. House of Representatives," *American Political Science Review* 62 (March 1968): 144–68.

15. Barnes, in Rose, pp. 171–226; Vittorio Capecchi, V. Cioni Polacchini, G. Galli, and G. Sivini, *Il comportamento elettorale in Italia* (Bologna: Il Mulino, 1968); Galli and Prandi; Perpaolo Luzzatto Fegiz, *Il volto sconosciuto dell'Italia, 1946–1956*; and Luzzatto Fegiz, *Il volto sconosciuto dell'Italia, seconda serie, 1956–1965* (Milano: Giuffre, 1957 and 1966); and Gianfranco Poggi, *Le preferenze politiche degli italiani: analisi di alcuni sondaggi preelettorali* (Bologna: Il Mulino, 1968).

16. Robert Putnam, *Beliefs of Politicians: Ideology, Conflict, and Democracy in Britain and Italy* (New Haven, Conn.: Yale University Press, 1973), p. 193. Devotion to the constitution was evident in the interviews of Gordon J. DiRenzo with Italian Communist deputies, though his interpretation differed from the viewpoint expressed by Putnam and by the present author. DiRenzo, *Personality, Power, and Politics* (South Bend, Ind.: University of Notre Dame Press, 1967).

17. As used by Emeric Deutsch, Denis Lindon, and Pierre Weill, *Les familles politiques aujourd'hui en France* (Paris: Les Editions de Minuit, 1966).

18. Harold D. Lasswell and Abraham Kaplan, *Power and Society* (New Haven, Conn.: Yale University Press, 1950), p. 123. They continue, "We call a pattern of political symbols a utopia if their function in the political process is to induce fundamental changes in power relationships or practices, an ideology, if they serve to maintain the given power patterns." Thus the Neofascists are currently utopian in many respects. This analysis is developed by Karl Mannheim in *Ideology and Utopia* (New York: Harcourt, Brace, 1936).

19. Robert N. Bellah, "Le cinque religioni dell'Italia moderna," in Fabio Luca Cavazza and Stephen R. Graubard, eds., *Il caso italiano* (Milan: Garzanti, 1974), pp. 439–68.

20. Croce's views are stated in *Storia d'Europa nel secolo XIX* (Bari: Laterza, 1972 (1st ed. 1932).

21. Bellah, p. 441.

22. Gramsci's views are stated in *Il materialismo storico e la filosofia di Benedetto Croce* (Turin: Einaudi, 1948).

23. On this point the views of Francesco Alberoni on the historical role of the church in institutionalizing charisma and virtually causing the development of a hierarchical and elite-dominated politics in Italy are of particular relevance; see Alberoni, "Carisma d'ufficio e movimenti spontanei," in Cavazza and Graubard, pp. 469–76.

24. Bellah claims that in purely religious terms it is emotional rather than rational, particularistic, animistic, it worships Mary more as an earth-mother figure than as the Mother of God, and it views the Catholic hierarchy more as an expression of traditional than of religious authority. Bellah views this pre-christian religion as a stratum underlying the other religions, one that affects more what people do than what they believe. He uses the musical metaphor of the "basso continuo" to suggest "a deep and repetitive resonance, an accompanying base that continues regardless of the melodic developments of the higher registers (theology and formal philosophy), at times drowning them out completely" (p. 444). Bellah believes that such an underlying stratum of beliefs exists everywhere, but that it is more intense in some countries than in others, for example, in Japan than China and in Italy than in France or England.

25. The best general interpretation of the evolution of the Italian party system is Giorgio Galli's *I partiti politici in Italia, 1861–1973* (Torino: UTET, 1975). The early period has been widely studied. Good introductions in English include the following: Dennis Mack Smith, *Italy* (Ann Arbor: The University of Michigan Press, 1969); A. J. Whyte, *The Evolution of Modern Italy* (New York: Norton, 1965); René Albrecht-Carrie, *Italy from Napoleon to Mussolini* (New York: Columbia University Press, 1960); Raymond Grew, *A Sterner Plan for Italian Unity* (Princeton, N.J.: Princeton University Press, 1963); Christopher Seton-Watson, *Italy from Liberalism to Fascism* (London: Methuen, 1967); Benedetto Croce, *A History of Italy, 1871–1915* (Oxford: Oxford University Press, 1929); and A. William Salomone, *Italy in the Giolittian Era: Italian Democracy in the Making, 1900–1914*, 2d ed. (Philadelphia: University of Pennsylvania Press, 1960).

26. Apart from numerous biographies of Mussolini, there are several useful works on the Fascists: Angelo Tasca, *The Rise of Italian Fascism 1918–1922* (London: Methuen, 1938); Charles F. Delzell, *Mussolini's Enemies: The Italian Anti-Fascist Resistance* (Princeton, N.J.: Princeton University Press, 1961);

Dante Germino, *The Italian Fascist Party in Power; A Study in Totalitarian Rule* (Minneapolis: University of Minnesota Press, 1959); Webster, (see n. 3 above); and A. J. Gregor, *The Ideology of Fascism* (New York: Free Press, 1969). The best work is still under way by Renzo DeFelice, and thus far three volumes have been published by Einaudi of Turin: *Mussolini il rivoluzionario* (1965); *Mussolini il fascista: la conquista del potere, 1921–1925* (1966); and *Mussolini il fascista: l'organizzazione dello stato fascista, 1925–1929* (1968). See also Gregor's essay, "On Understanding Fascism: A Review of Some Contemporary Literature," *American Political Science Review* 67 (December 1973): 1332–47.

27. See Samuel H. Barnes, "The Legacy of Fascism: Generational Differences in Italian Political Attitudes and Behavior," *Comparative Political Studies* 5 (April 1972): 41–58. Readers interested in this article should write the author for a corrected version; the published article includes the text from one draft and the tables from another, so it will be unintelligible!

28. A. F. K. Organski, *The Stages of Political Development* (New York: Knopf, 1965).

29. This has been analyzed elsewhere; see Alan Arian and Samuel H. Barnes, "The Dominant Party System: A Neglected Model of Democratic Stability," *Journal of Politics* 36 (August 1974): 592–614.

NOTES TO CHAPTER THREE

1. Vittorio Capecchi, V. Cioni Polacchini, G. Galli, and G. Sivini, *Il comportamento elettorale in Italia* (Bologna: Il Mulino, 1968), p. 23.

2. Ibid., pp. 69–70.

3. Luigi D'Amato, *Il voto di preferenza in Italia* (Milano: Giuffre, 1964).

4. Giovanni Schepis, "Analisi statistica dei risultati," in Alberto Spreafico and Joseph LaPalombara, eds., *Elezioni e comportamento politico in Italia* (Milano: Communità, 1963, table 26).

5. Rae, pp. 120, 105 (see chap. 1, n. 13).

6. Ibid., p. 120.

NOTES TO CHAPTER FOUR

1. See, for example, the analyses in Richard Rose, ed., *Electoral Behavior: A Comparative Handbook* (New York: Free Press, 1974). They demonstrate the widespread importance of social networks.

2. See John A. Sonquist and James N. Morgan, *The Detection of Interaction Effects,* (Ann Arbor, Mich.: Survey Research Center, 1964). The particular variety of tree analysis used here is that of DATUM-INFAS of Bad Godesberg, Germany, which is similar to the program described in Sonquist and Morgan, with one important difference. That is that the Sonquist-Morgan program automatically chooses the variables and dichotomization of the variables that explain the greatest portion of the total variance, while the DATUM-INFAS program permits the analyst to select the division at each branch that seems most relevant theoretically. For example, in the analysis that follows this option was used once—in selecting geographical subdivisions. Northeast Italy, northwest Italy, and central Italy formed a unit; while southern Italy and the islands *plus* Lombardy, which is treated as a separate geographical area, formed another unit, with this arrangement explaining 1.7 percent of the total

variance. However, by taking the division with the second greatest explanatory power, which was similar to the above with the exception that Lombardy was in the northern rather than southern set, the total variance explained was 1.5 percent, which is not a great cost to pay in explanatory power considering the theoretical simplicity it brings to the analysis.

3. A note of caution is necessary because of the severe underrepresentation of the PCI identifiers. Of the total sample, 20.7 percent did not express a preference for any party. Only 12.4 percent listed the PCI, though that party received 26.9 percent of the 1968 vote. It is probable that PCI identifiers were more likely than others to refuse to be interviewed. Among the completed interviews, a superficial analysis of the nonidentifiers suggests that the PCI portion of this group is somewhat greater than its portion of the total vote, but it also leads to the tentative conclusion that the remaining PCI identifiers are hidden in the vote for other parties as well. If true, this would attenuate the strength of the findings; hence, better identification of PCI voters should greatly increase the explanatory power of the analysis. A comment is also needed concerning the meaning of the variable of church attendance. It may be measuring actual church attendance, or it may be measuring psychological identification with the Catholic subculture; that is, it may merely elicit what in the subculture is the "right" answer concerning church attendance. The percentage claiming weekly church attendance may seem high, but it is similar to findings reported by Almond and Verba and DOXA. In the Five Nation Study, 57 percent claimed weekly church attendance (Gabriel Almond and Sidney Verba, *The Civic Culture Codebook*, [Ann Arbor, Mich.: ICPSR, n.d.] p. 111). DOXA reported 69 percent (Pierpaolo Luzzatto Fegiz, *Il volto sconosciuto dell'Italia, seconda serie, 1956–1965* p. 1283; see chap. 2, n. 15). Scattered local studies of church attendance based on parish head counts suggest that these figures may be inflated. Nevertheless, in the absence of more compelling evidence, weekly church attendance will be interpreted as indicating, at the very least, deep involvement in the communication network of the Catholic subculture.

4. These scores are based on a sympathy scale; each respondent gave a score that went from 0 (negative) to 100 (positive), with 50 as a neutral point.

5. Stefano Passigli, *Emigrazione e comportamento politico* (Bologna: Il Mulino, 1969), pp. 18, 21.

6. See Giovanni Sartori, et al., *Il parlamento italiano* (Napoli: Edizioni Scientifiche, 1963), for an extended analysis of the background of Italian parliamentarians.

7. The generational problem is quite serious for the DC. Among those aged 21–29, 44 percent identify with the DC; 30–39, 51 percent; 40–49, 52 percent; 50–59, 52 percent; 60–69, 60 percent; 70–79, 63 percent; and 80 and over, 75 percent. If population replacement were the sole source of electoral change the DC could expect a sharp decline in the decade after the 1968 survey, followed by relative stability due to the similarity of its level of support in the age 30–59 categories. But while population replacement is probably the most important single source of change, other forces are at work. Furthermore, the small size of the sample and especially the severe underrepresentation of the PCI identifiers make it dangerous to extend this type of analysis very far. For an example of what can be done with this type of analysis, see David Butler and Donald

Stokes, *Political Change in Britain* (New York: St. Martin's, 1969), chaps. 11–13. Using data from the 1968 and 1972 surveys, plus demographic materials, Giacomo Sani has demonstrated that time strongly favors the Italian left; see "Secular Trends and Party Realignments in Italy: the 1975 election" (paper prepared for delivery at the 1975 annual meeting of the American Political Science Association, San Francisco, September 2–5, 1975). Of course, much depends on the response of the DC to the challenge.

NOTES TO CHAPTER FIVE

1. Seymour M. Lipset and Stein Rokkan, "Cleavage Structures, Party Systems, and Voter Alignments: An Introduction," in Lipset and Rokkan, pp. 1–64, at p. 50 (see chap. 1, n. 12).

2. See Anne Foner, "The Polity," in Matilda W. Riley, Marilyn Johnson, and Anne Foner, eds., *Aging and Society* (New York: Russell Sage Foundation, 1972), pp. 115–59; and Herbert H. Hyman, *Secondary Analysis of Sample Surveys: Principles, Procedures and Potentialities* (New York: Wiley, 1972), pp. 257–90. There is also a vast literature that deals in particular with age differences in partisanship in the United States; for examples, see John Crittenden, "Aging and Party Affiliation: A Cohort Analysis," *Public Opinion Quarterly* 26 (Winter 1962): 648–57; Neal Cutler, "Generation, Maturation and Party Affiliation," *Public Opinion Quarterly* 33 (Winter 1969): 583–89; and Norval D. Glenn and Ted Hefner, "Further Evidence on Aging and Party Identification," *Public Opinion Quarterly* 36 (Spring 1972): 31–47.

3. David Butler and Donald Stokes, *Political Change in Britain* (New York: St. Martins, 1969), p. 59.

4. Vittorio Capecchi, V. Cioni Polacchini, G. Galli, and G. Sivini used aggregate data to demonstrate this in *Il comportamento elettorale in Italia* (Bologna: Il Mulino, 1968), pp. 245–46.

5. Samuel H. Barnes and Giacomo Sani have shown that new parties had great difficulty penetrating the electorate in the 1972 elections. See "Nuovi movimenti politici e partiti tradizionali," in Mario Caciagli and Alberto Spreafico, eds., *Un sistema politico all prova* (Bologna: Il Mulino, 1975), pp. 153–78.

6. This point is developed by T. Allen Lambert, "Generations and Change: Toward a Theory of Generations as a Force in Historical Process," *Youth and Society* 4 (September 1972): 21–46.

7. Samuel H. Barnes and Giacomo Sani, "Mediterranean Political Culture and Italian Politics: An Interpretation," *British Journal of Political Science* 4 (July 1974): 289–303.

8. Johan Galtung, *Members of Two Worlds* (New York: Columbia University Press, 1971), 190–91.

9. See Ronald Inglehart, "The Silent Revolution in Europe: Intergenerational Change in Post-Industrial Societies," *American Political Science Review* 65 (December 1971): 991–1017, and *The Silent Revolution: Changing Values and Political Styles among Western Publics* (Princeton: Princeton University Press, 1977).

10. On this point see Orville G. Brim, Jr. and Stanton Wheeler, *Socialization After Childhood* (New York: Wiley, 1966), and Donald Searing, Gerald Wright, and George Rabinowitz, "The Primacy Principle: Attitude Change and

Political Socialization," *British Journal of Political Science* 6 (January 1976): 83–113.

11. The American evidence is summarized in R. W. Connell, "Political Socialization in the American Family: The Evidence Re-examined," *Public Opinion Quarterly* 36 (Fall 1972): 323–33. For a more general summary of this literature plus citations, see Richard E. Dawson and Kenneth Prewitt, *Political Socialization* (Boston: Little, Brown, 1969), pp. 44–52, 105–26.

12. Philip E. Converse and Georges Dupeux, "Politicization of the Electorate in France and the United States," in Angus Campbell, Philip E. Converse, Warren E. Miller, and Donald E. Stokes, *Elections and the Political Order* (New York: Wiley, 1966), pp. 269–91.

13. Ibid.

14. Ibid., p. 291. Subsequent changes in partisanship in France and the United States indicate the temporal nature of social science findings. In 1972, Ronald Inglehart and Avram Hochstein presented data indicating that in 1968—ten years after the Converse and Dupeux surveys—69 percent of the American respondents reported a partisan preference, compared with 76 percent in 1958, while the French percentage had grown from 56 percent in 1956 to 84 percent in 1968! "Alignment and Dealignment of the Electorate in France and the United States," *Comparative Political Studies* 5 (October 1972): 349, 353.

15. Philip Converse, "Of Time and Partisan Stability," *Comparative Political Studies* 2 (July 1969): 148.

16. The 1959 data are from ICPSR, *Five-Nation Study;* the 1959 figure includes those who claimed past or present party membership or who supported or leaned toward a particular party; 1968 data are from the current representation study.

17. Converse, "Of Time and Partisan Stability," p. 149.

18. Ibid., p. 163.

19. Voting continuity is probably greater than indicated. Barnes and Giacomo Sani executed a national survey in 1972 in which 78 percent claimed to have *always* voted for the same party and 86 percent said that they had voted for the same party in both 1968 and 1972. Because of the PSI-PSDI division into two parties plus the merger of the MSI and Monarchists, both of which took place between 1968 and 1972, many respondents probably classified themselves as switchers when they were in fact quite constant. The actual continuity in voting between the two elections must have been even higher. The 1972 survey was made possible by grants to the ISR, of the University of Michigan, and the Ohio State University from the Ford Foundation and the National Science Foundation. The survey was conducted by Fieldwork, S.R.L. of Milan following the political elections of 1972.

20. See n. 19.

21. Sani, "Political Traditions as Contextual Variables: Partisanship in Italy," *American Journal of Political Science* 20 (August 1976): 375–405.

22. Ibid., pp. 379–80.

23. Ibid., p. 381.

24. Ibid., pp. 390–91.

25. Ibid., p. 391.

26. Capecchi et al., p. 100.

27. When partisan preference is regressed on traditions, organizational affiliation, and father's party preference, Beta for Catholic tradition in 1946 is .001 and for Socialist tradition in 1946 is -.075. Beta for ties with left organizations is -.279; for ties with Catholic organizations, .091; for church attendance, .187; and for party preference of father, it is .398. R is .681. (Sani, table 10, p. 399)

NOTES TO CHAPTER SIX
1. Almond and Verba (see chap. 2, n. 5).
2. Milbrath (see chap. 1, n. 11).
3. Verba and Nie (see chap. 1, n. 11).
4. Converse (see chap. 5, no. 15).
5. Milbrath, pp. 134–35; see also Norman H. Nie, Sidney Verba, and Jae-on Kim, "Political Participation and the Life Cycle," *Comparative Politics* 6 (April 1974): 319–40.
6. Milbrath, p. 56.
7. How structural factors favor working-class rather than middle-class partisanship in Norway is explored by Angus Campbell and Stein Rokkan, "Citizen Participation in Political Life: Norway and the U.S." *International Social Science Journal* 12 (1960): 69–99.
8. Samuel H. Barnes, "Participation, Education, and Political Competence: Evidence from a Sample of Italian Socialists," *American Political Science Review* 60 (June 1966): 348–53.

NOTES TO CHAPTER SEVEN
1. Harold Hotelling, "Stability in Competition," *Economic Journal* 39 (1929): 41–57.
2. Arthur Smithies, "Optimum Location in Spatial Competition," *Journal of Political Economy* 49 (1941): 423–39.
3. Anthony Downs, *An Economic Theory of Democracy* (New York: Harper & Brothers, 1957), esp. chap. 8, pp. 114–141; see also Jean A. Laponce, "Note on the Use of the Left-Right Dimension," *Comparative Political Studies* 2 (January 1970): 481–502; Giovanni Sartori, "Modelli spaziali di competizione tra partiti," *Rassegna italiana di sociologia* 6 (January–March 1965): 7–29; and Hans D. Klingemann, "Testing the Left-Right Continuum on a Sample of German Voters," *Comparative Political Studies* 5 (April 1972): 93–106.
4. Downs.
5. Several scholars have argued that left-right placement of self and of the parties represents a labeling device used by respondents to simplify a complex party space. That is, left and right are not ideologically derived by the respondent as an aid in the selection of party but rather are simply aspects of the party label, acquired along with ties to party, and, like ties to party, reflecting complex patterns of explanation. Thus left and right would be ideological only to the extent that party attachment is truly ideological. For examples of this view see Giacomo Sani, "A Test of the Least-Distance Model of Voting Choice: Italy, 1972," *Comparative Political Studies* 7 (July 1974): 193–208; and Ronald Inglehart and Hans D. Klingemann, "Party Identification, Ideological Preference and the Left-Right Dimension among Western Mass Publics," in Ian Budge, Ivor Crewe and Dennis Farlie (eds.), *Party Identification and Beyond*

(London and New York: Wiley, 1976), 243–73. This explanation is undoubtedly adequate for a substantial portion of the population. But it requires that people learn different left-right placements for the same parties; otherwise, members of the same party would not be as spread out as they are in fig. 4. This is, of course, quite possible, as the parties are perceived differently in different areas and in different milieus. Likewise difficult to accommodate to this thesis is the fact that many respondents do not place themselves and their parties exactly similarly. They may think of themselves as being to the left or the right of their parties. With the data available we cannot unravel these knots.

6. "Spatial Models of Party Competition," in Angus Campbell, P. E. Converse, W. E. Miller, and D. E. Stokes, *Elections and the Political Order* (New York: Wiley, 1966), esp. pp. 165–76.

7. See Barnes and Sani, "Nuovi movimenti politici e partiti tradizionali" (see chap. 5, n. 5); and Barnes and Sani, "Partisan Change and the Italian Voter: Some Clues from the 1972 Election" (paper prepared for delivery at the International Political Science Association Congress, Montreal, August 1973).

8. Stokes, p. 173.

9. Herbert McClosky, "Consensus and Ideology in American Politics," *American Political Science Review* 58 (June 1964): 361–79.

10. Samuel H. Barnes, *Party Democracy*, pp. 167–72 (see chap. 1, n. 10).

11. This is perhaps the reason why the perceptions of the Monarchist identifiers fit so poorly with the conventional wisdom: They are the most uninformed and clientelistic of the party identifiers. It is likely that the conventional wisdom's placement of the party reflects accurately the attitudes of its elite. Unfortunately, we have no measures of MON elite attitudes to confirm or deny this hunch.

NOTES TO CHAPTER EIGHT

1. On the 1974 referendum, see Alberto Marradi, "Analisi del referendum sul divorzio," *Rivista italiana di scienza politica* 4 (December 1974): 589–644.

2. This will be demonstrated in Chapter 9.

3. Sidney Verba and Norman H. Nie, pp. 71, 75 (see chap. 1, n. 11).

NOTES TO CHAPTER NINE

1. For an introduction see David R. Hager and Manindra K. Mohapatra, *Cross-National Legislative Institutions, Processes, and Behavior: A Bibliography* (Norfolk, Va.: Old Dominion University, Department of Political Science, 1974).

2. Donald Searing, "The Comparative Study of Elite Socialization," *Comparative Political Studies* 1 (January 1969): 471–500.

3. *Il parlamento italiano, 1946–1963* (Napoli: Edizioni Scientifiche Italiane, 1963).

4. For an introduction to this topic see Raphael Zariski, "Intra-Party Conflict in a Dominant Party: The Experience of Italian Christian Democracy," *Journal of Politics* 27 (February 1965): 19–34; Zariski, "The Italian Socialist Party: A Case Study in Factional Conflict," *American Political Science Review* 56 (June 1962): 372–90; Franco Cazzola, "Partiti, correnti, e voto di preferenza," *Rivista italiana di scienza politica* 2 (December 1972): 569–88; Cazzola, *Il partito come organizzazione-studio di un caso: il PSI*, Rome: Edizioni del Tritone, 1970;

Cazzola, *Carisma e democrazia nel socialismo italiano*, Rome: Istituto Luigi Sturzo, 1967; Giovanni Sartori, "Proporzionalismo, frazionismo, e crisi dei partiti," *Rivista italiano di scienza politica* 1 (December 1971): 629–55; Stefano Passigli, "Proporzionalismo, frazionismo, e crisi dei partiti: quid prior?" *Rivista italiana di scienza politica* 2 (April 1972): 125–38; Antonio Lombardo, "Dal proporzionalismo intrapartitico al fazionismo eterodiretto," *Rivista italiana di scienza politica* 2 (August 1972): 369–81; and Gianfranco Pasquino, "Le radici del frazionismo e il voto di preferenza," *Rivista italiana di scienza politica* 2 (August 1972): 353–68.

NOTES TO CHAPTER TEN

1. Robert Michels, *Political Parties* (New York: Dover 1959; the original German edition was published in 1911); S. M. Lipset, James Coleman, and Martin From, *Union Democracy* (Garden City, N.J.: Doubleday, 1962); Samuel J. Eldersveld, *Political Parties: A Behavioral Analysis* (Chicago: Rand McNally, 1964); Henry Valen and Daniel Katz, *Political Parties in Norway* (Oslo: Universitetsforlaget, 1964); Renate Mayntz, "Oligarchic Problems in German Party Districts," in Dwaine Marvick ed., *Political Decisionmakers: Recruitment and Performance* (New York: Free Press, 1961), pp. 138–92; Robert T. McKenzie, *British Political Parties* (New York: St. Martin's, 1955); and Samuel H. Barnes, *Party Democracy* (see chap. 1, n. 10).

2. Albert O. Hirschman, *Exit, Voice, and Loyalty*, (Cambridge, Mass.: Harvard University Press, 1970).

Index

Action Party, 140
Administration of elections, 34
Agricultural population, 55–56
Alberoni, Francesco, 174
Albrecht-Carrie, René, 174
Alienation, 18
Allardt, Erik, 172
Almond, Gabriel, 163, 171, 173, 176, 179
Amicable agreement, 19
Amoral familism, 9
Anarchism, 28
Area differences, 55, 57, 154
Arian, Alan, 175
Aristocracy, 56

Banfield, Edward, 9, 168, 169
Banton, Michael, 168
Barber, J. D., 170
Barnes, Samuel H., 69, 76, 93, 108, 168, 173, 175, 177, 178, 179, 180, 181
Bellah, Robert N., 23, 24, 174
Bill, James A., 169
Birch, Anthony H., 167
Blondel, Jean, 170
Bolshevik revolution, 26
Brim, Orville G., Jr., 177
Buchanan, William, 170

Budge, Ian, 179
Bureaucracy, 29–30
Burke, Edmund, 11
Butler, David, 66, 176, 177

Caciagli, Mario, 177
Campaign: nomination, 36, 38, 144–55; preference votes, 16, 146–50; recognition of candidates, 94–96; role of mass media, 149
Campbell, Angus, 178, 179, 180
Capecchi, Vittorio, 173, 175, 177, 178
Catholicism in Italy: Catholic Action, 54; Catholic subculture, 51, 53; clergy, 55; general, 15, 17, 21, 23, 24, 25, 27, 28, 53, 72–73, 102; social program, 57; traditions, 24, 25, 72, 159
Cazzola, Franco, 171, 180–81
Chamber of Deputies, 16, 20, 33, 36
Chapman, John W., 167
Christian Democratic Party (DC), 12, 13, 15, 16, 19, 20, 21, 26, 28, 29, 30, 36, 38, 51, 53, 55, 58, 66, 72–73, 74, 100, 113, 120, 124, 143, 158
Church attendance, 42, 44, 50
Clientelism (patron-client system), 7, 8, 9, 24, 28, 29, 30, 125, 135
Coleman, James, 181

Communist Party (PCI), 12, 15–16, 19, 21, 26–27, 31–32, 38, 49, 55, 58, 74, 100, 102, 104, 120, 124, 164
Confederaziona italiana sindacati nazionale lavoratori (CISNAL), 53–54
Confederazione generale italiana del lavoro (CGIL), 42, 44, 54
Confederazione italiana sindacati lavoratori (CISL), 53, 54
Connell, R. W., 178
Consociational democracy, 19
Converse, Philip E., 71, 72, 81, 178, 179, 180
Corporatism, 7
Crewe, Ivor, 179
Crittenden, John, 177
Croce, Benedetto, 23, 24, 174
Cutler, Neal, 177
Cutright, Philips, 170

Daadler, Hans, 18, 169, 173
D'Amato, Luigi, 175
DATUM-INFAS, 175
Dawson, Richard E., 178
DeFelice, Renzo, 175
de Gaspari, Alcide, 12
De Grazia, Alfred, 2, 167
Delzell, Charles F., 174
Democratic centralism, 32, 143
Deputies: elective public offices held, 142–43; how they should vote, 129; joining the party, 137–40; occupations, 58; previous party affiliations, 140; social class, 58
Deutsch, Emeric, 173
Diaz, May N., 168
DiPalma, Giuseppe, 170, 171
Direct Cultivators (coltivatori diretti), 30, 152, 154
DiRenzo, Gordon J., 173
Divorce movement, 120
Downs, Anthony, 98–99, 179
Dupeux, Georges, 71, 178
Dye, Thomas R., 170

Education, 61–67; political effects of, 61, 63, 64, 67

Eldersveld, Samuel J., 181
Elections, 12, 33, 34, 37, 150–55
Elites, 19, 29
Emigration, 56
Eulau, Heinz, 11, 14, 167, 170, 171

Factory committees, 141
Falconi, Carlo, 172
Familles politiques, 21
Farlie, Dennis, 179
Fascism, 23, 26–27, 29–30
Ferguson, Leroy, 170
Ferrari, Pierre, 171
Fiorina, Morris P., 170
Foner, Anne, 177
Foster, George, 168
Franchi tiratori, 14
From, Martin, 181

Galli, Giorgio, 15, 171, 173–75, 177–78
Galtung, Johan, 177
Generation effects, 66
Generation gap, 67
Germino, Dante, 175
Giustizia e Libertà, 140
Glenn, Norval D., 177
Gramsci, Antonio, 23, 174
Graubard, Stephen R., 174
Graziano, Luigi, 169
Greenstein, Fred I., 168
Gregor, A. J., 175
Grew, Raymond, 174

Hager, David R., 180
Hallowell, John H., 173
Hancock, M. Donald, 169
Hefner, Ted, 177
Heisler, Martin O., 172
Hinckley, Katherine, 11, 170
Hirsch, Herbert, 169
Hirschman, Albert O., 158, 181
Historic Compromise, 19
Hochstein, Avram, 178
Hofferbert, Richard I., 170
Holt, Robert T., 169
Horowitz, D. L., 172
Hotelling, Harold, 98, 179

House of Representatives, U.S., 20
Huntington, Samuel P., 18, 169, 172, 173
Hyman, Herbert H., 177

Ideology, 23, 25, 29, 31
Inglehart, Ronald, 177, 178, 179
Institutionalization, 17, 18, 24, 66
Inter-university Consortium for Political and Social Research, 178

Jemolo, Arturo Carlo, 172
Jewell, Malcolm E., 170
Johnson, Marilyn, 177

Kaplan, Abraham, 22, 174
Katz, Daniel, 181
Kim, Jae-on, 168, 171, 179
Klingemann, Hans D., 179
Kornberg, Allen, 169, 170, 171
Kvavik, Robert B., 172

Lambert, T. Allen, 177
LaPalombara, Joseph, 169, 170, 172, 175
Laponce, Jean A., 179
Lasswell, Harold D., 22, 174
Lateran treaties, 27
Left and right in Italy, 22, 23, 104, 109
Legg, Kenneth, 168
Legislatures, 11, 15
Lehmbruch, Gerhard, 173
Lemarchand, René, 168
Lewin, Kurt, 100
Liberal Party (PLI), 12, 28, 30, 55
Liberalism, 23, 25, 56
Life-cycle effects, 66
Lijphart, Arend, 173
Lindon, Denis, 173
Lipset, S. M., 10, 65, 168, 177, 181
Littunen, Yrjo, 172
Loewenberg, Gerard, 1, 11, 15, 167, 169, 170, 171, 172
Lombardo, Antonio, 181
Lorwin, Val, 173
Lotti, Luigi, 136
Luca Cavazza, Fabio, 174

Luzzatto Fegiz, Pierpaulo, 173, 176

McCloskey, Herbert, 108, 180
McKenzie, Robert T., 181
Mack Smith, Dennis, 174
MacRae, Duncan, Jr., 170
MacRae, Kenneth, 173
Maisl, Herbert, 171
Mannheim, Karl, 22
Manoukian, Agopik, 173
Maranini, Giuseppe, 171
Marradi, Alberto, 180
Marvick, Dwaine, 181
Marx, Karl, 23
Mayntz, Renate, 181
Meynaud, Jean, 172
Michels, Robert, 181
Middle class, 56, 57
Milbrath, Lester, 3, 79, 89, 168, 179
Miller, Warren E., 15, 170, 172, 178, 180
Mobilization, 2, 5, 29, 157–58
Mohapatra, Manindra, 180
Monarchist parties, 28, 36, 58
Monarchy, 28, 159
Moore, Barrington, Jr., 169
Morgan, James N., 175
Musolf, Lloyd, 169, 170

National Right (*Destra Nazionale*), 30
Nettl, J. P., 167
Nie, Norman, 3, 79, 125, 168, 169, 171, 179, 180

Opening to the Left, 12–13, 26
Organski, A. F. K., 29, 175

Parliament, 14, 16, 20, 32
Partisan stability, model of, 71
Partisanship: continuity of, 65, 71, 74, 75, 76–77; effect of contextual variables, 76–77; and father's identification, 71, 74, 75
Party democracy, 158
Party: elites, occupational composition, 58; factions, 143–44; identification, 38, 45, 53, 109, 112; organization, 28–29, 135

Pasquino, Gianfranco, 173, 181
Passigli, Stefano, 176, 181
Patterson, Samuel, C., 170
Pennock, J. Roland, 167
Period effects, 66
Personal efficacy, measurement of, 90
Pitkin, Hannah, 167
Pitt-Rivers, Julian, 168
Poggi, Gianfranco, 172, 173
Polacchini, V. Cioni, 173, 175, 177, 178
Political class, 57
Political cleavage, dimensions of, 10, 41
Political culture, 69
Political efficacy, measurement of, 90
Poitical involvement, 3, 78–87; and age, 82–83; and church attendance, 88–89; and education, 85–87; and geographical area, 84–85; and network ties, 87–89; and occupational status, 85; party differences in, 80–81; and political knowledge, 93; and psychological indicators, 91–93; and sex differences, 81–82; and size of commune, 87; and strength of partisanship, 81; typology of, 79; union ties, 88
Poitical knowledge, party names, 94
Political mobilization, patterns of, 78
Political participation, 3
Political socialization, 70
Political traditions, 66, 157
Political trust, measures of, 90
Polsby, Nelson W., 168, 170, 173
Pope John XXIII, 51
Popular party, 28, 29
Population replacement model of electoral change, 69
Position issues, 100, 110, 119
Potter, Jack M., 168
Powell, G. Bingham, Jr., 173
Prandi, Alfonso, 15, 171, 172, 173
Predieri, Alberto, 136
Prefect, 29
Press, 149
Prewitt, Kenneth, 14, 167, 171, 178
Prime minister, 29

Problems facing Italy, 124
Proportional representation, 16, 35
Proporzdemokratie, 19
Putnam, Robert, 6, 21, 168, 173

Rabinowitz, George, 177
Rae, Douglas, 37, 168, 175
Ranney, Austin, 170
Referendum: on monarchy, 159; on repeal of divorce law, 33, 120, 159
Religious practice, 49–50
Representation, 1, 4, 14, 15, 150, 156; beliefs as linkage, 117; class interests as linkage, 117; constituency linkages, 121; contacts as linkages, 125–28; contacts with deputies or senators, 126, 127; isomorphism in social background as linkage, 116; issue agreement as linkage, 118–25; normative evaluations of roles, 128–33; party offices held, 140–42; political careers, 136–43
Republican Party (PRI), 13, 25, 26, 28, 31, 36, 55
Revisionism, 32
Riley, Matilda, 177
Risé, Claudio, 172
Robinson, James A., 170
Rokkan, Stein, 10, 65, 168, 172, 177, 179
Roll-call votes in Italian Parliament, 117–18
Rose, Richard, 168, 173, 175

Salomone, A. William, 174
Samples, 163
Sani, Giacomo, 69, 76, 177, 178, 179, 180
Sartori, Giovanni, 2, 11, 14, 58, 136, 137, 167, 170, 176, 179, 181
Schepis, Giovanni, 175
Schorger, William D., 168
Scott, James C., 169
Searing, Donald, 177, 180
Segmented pluralism, 19
Senate, 33, 36
Sense of personal efficacy, measures of, 91

Sense of political efficacy, measures of, 90
Seton-Watson, Christopher, 174
Settembrini, Domenico, 172
Sex differences, 44, 55, 57, 81
Shannon, Wayne, 170
Sivini, Giordano, 173, 175, 177, 178
Smithies, Arthur, 98, 179
Social class, *borghesia*, 57
Social Democratic Party (PSDI), 13, 16, 26, 58
Social Movement (MSI), 28–30, 55, 58
Social networks, 42, 44, 49
Socialist Party (PSI), 12, 16, 26, 28, 31, 32, 55, 104, 108, 143
Socialist Party of Proletarian Unity (PSIUP), 31, 55
Socialist Party–Social Democratic Party (PSI-PSDI), 31, 55, 120, 124, 164
Somogyi, S., 136
Sonquist, John A., 175
Sottogoverno, 13
Spatial models, 97–101, 106–15
Spreafico, Alberto, 175, 177
Steiner, Jürg, 173
Stokes, Donald E., 15, 66, 99, 100, 170, 172, 176, 177, 178, 180
Study design, 163–65
Styskal, Richard A., 169
Subjective social class, 60
Südtiroler Volkspartei, 36
Suffrage, Extension of, 25
Systemic Representation, 122

Tarrow, Sidney, 168, 169
Tasca, Angelo, 174

Taylor, Michael, 168
Traditions in Italy, 15, 18, 19, 23, 24, 25, 28, 56
Trasformismo, 29
Tree analysis, 42
Trust, measurement of, 90
Turner, John E., 169
Turner, Julius, 170

Unions, 53, 54, 141
Utopia, 23, 25–26

Valen, Henry, 181
Valence issues, 100, 110, 119
Vatican, 20, 27
Verba, Sidney, 3, 79, 125, 163, 168, 169, 171, 173, 176, 179, 180
Vogelin, Eric, 167
Voting, 34, 37

Wahlke, J. C., 170, 171
Webster, Richard A., 172, 175
Weill, Pierre, 173
Weiner, Myron, 169
Wheeler, Stanton, 177
Whyte, A. J., 174
Wolf, Eric R., 168
Women, political role of, 67
Women's organizations, 141
Wright, Gerald, 177

Youth organizations, 141

Zariski, Raphael, 180
Zuckerman, Alan, 8, 169